THE LIFE AND TIMES OF JESUS

MICHAEL J. RUSZALA

© Wyatt North Publishing, LLC 2014

Publishing by Wyatt North Publishing, LLC. A Boutique Publishing Company.

"Wyatt North" and "A Boutique Publishing Company" are trademarks of Wyatt North Publishing, LLC.

Copyright © Wyatt North Publishing, LLC. All rights reserved, including the right to reproduce this book or portions thereof in any form whatsoever. For more information please visit http://www.WyattNorth.com.

Cover design by Wyatt North Publishing, LLC. Copyright © Wyatt North Publishing, LLC. All rights reserved.

Scripture texts in this work are taken from the *New American Bible, revised edition*© 2010, 1991, 1986, 1970 Confraternity of Christian Doctrine, Washington, D.C. and are used by permission of the copyright owner. All Rights Reserved. No part of the New American Bible may be reproduced in any form without permission in writing from the copyright owner.

About Wyatt North Publishing

Starting out with just one writer, Wyatt North Publishing has expanded to include writers from across the country. Our writers include college professors, religious theologians, and historians.

Wyatt North Publishing provides high quality, perfectly formatted, original books.

Send us an email and we will personally respond within 24 hours! As a boutique publishing company we put our readers first and never respond with canned or automated emails. Send us an email at hello@WyattNorth.com, and you can visit us at www.WyattNorth.com.

About the Author

Michael J. Ruszala holds an M.A. in Theology & Christian Ministry and a B.A. in Philosophy and Theology *summa cum laude* from Franciscan University of Steubenville and is certified as a parish catechetical leader by the Diocese of Buffalo. He is director of faith formation at St. Pius X Catholic Church in Getzville, NY, and an adjunct lecturer in religious studies at Niagara University in Lewiston, NY. Michael is also an active member of the Society of Catholic Social Scientists and serves on the Catechumenate Board and the Faith Formation Assessment Committee for the Diocese of Buffalo. He has been published in several religious journals including the Social Justice Review, the Catholic Social Science Review, and Lay Witness online edition, with articles often touching on contemporary papal teaching. With interests in music, art, tennis, and kayaking, he also enjoys directing the Children's Choir at his parish.

Foreword	7
Introduction	11
Tensions from the Beginning	20
Proclaiming Victory over Evil	30
The Father and I Are One	40
Signs of God's Power	47
A Light to the Nations	57
The Lord's Prayer: Our Father in Heaven	63
The Lord's Prayer: Give Us This Day	71
The Crowds and the Believers	79
Rejection and Unbelief	87
The Approaching Hour	94
The Transfiguration	101
Jesus Enters Jerusalem	109
The Last Supper	117
Jesus Is Arrested	127
The Trial of Jesus	138
The Crucifixion of Jesus	148
The Sacrificial Death of Jesus	154
The Burial of Jesus	161
The Resurrection and Beyond	166
Epilogue	177

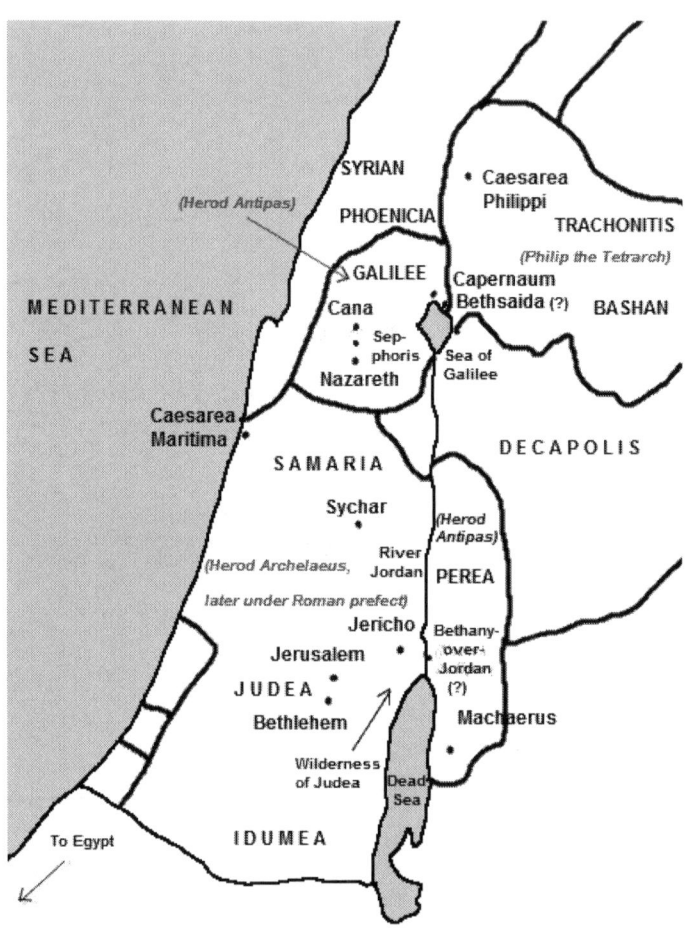

Foreword

Jesus was a Messiah behind enemy lines – God come into a sinful world ruled by evil. He was on a secret mission to save humanity. To Jesus' first-century Jewish contemporaries, whatever the Nazarene might be, he was not simply 'another good rabbi.' Jesus was a polarizing figure. One believed either that this powerful preacher and wonderworker was uniquely of God or that he was an agent of the Evil One. As he said in Luke's Gospel, "Whoever is not with me is against me, and whoever does not gather with me scatters" (Lk. 11:23).

We often speak of the love, mercy, and compassion of Jesus, but Malachi also prophesied of him, "Yes, he is coming, says the LORD of hosts. But who will endure the day of his coming? And who can stand when he appears? For he is like a refiner's fire" (Mal. 3:1-2). That is indeed how he came. Jesus was always moved by love of God and neighbor, but he was not always 'nice.' He was "meek and humble of heart" (Mt. 11:29) but never tame. Innocent though he was, it is little wonder that his boldness and zeal for righteousness provoked such powerful enemies; he knew it would be so. Jesus walked the earth at a time when human life had become cheapened, and prompt and brutal execution was a matter not so much of justice as of expedience. Ultimately, Jesus' paradoxical roles as fiery prophet and meek Lamb of God would intersect on the wood of the cross.

Jesus knew his enemy – Satan. He knew that, through Satan's tempting, humanity had fallen and now stood guilty before God, deprived of his grace. As St. Paul wrote in his Letter to the Romans, "For there is no distinction; all have sinned and are deprived of the glory of God" (Rom. 3:22). Jesus diagnosed the problems of the world as sin and the symptom as death, which came as a punishment for sin. His remedy, as God-man, was the shedding of his own blood in perfect obedience to the Father. His prognosis was suffering in the present but then, for those who are faithful, the unclouded glory of Heaven, where the Kingdom of God will finally reach its fullness. Thus, as is prayed in the Memorial Acclamation in the liturgy, "We proclaim your death O Lord and profess your Resurrection until you come again" (ICEL).

In these pages, we follow the path of Jesus as he enters ever deeper into the shadow of the cross. The Father's plan led through the cross to glory. In fact, to Jesus, whose mind was perfectly conformed to God's, the cross itself was glory since God's redeeming love was thereby revealed. Thus, it seems that as his 'hour' approached, Jesus boldly placed himself increasingly in harm's way, offering himself as a willing victim to repay, as God-man, what humanity could never offer on its own – an act of perfect obedience and infinite love.

Introduction

Jesus stands alone among the major religious founders of the world. There was Buddha, the 'Enlightened One,' who offered the way to nirvana. There was Mohammed, called the 'Prophet,' who directed his followers in how God wished to be served. There was Confucius, a wise teacher who showed people how to live. There was Moses, who spoke to God as a friend and mediated his presence to the people. But while Jesus was a prophet, teacher, and priestly mediator, he also uniquely claimed to *be* God. His key focus was bringing people to faith in *him*. Jesus *himself* was the message.

We read of Jesus in the Gospel of John, "In the beginning was the Word, and the Word was with God, and the Word was God" (Jn. 1:1). These words were written as early as AD 90. The Church has always taught Christ's divinity, confirming it at the Council of Nicaea in AD 325, but some have doubted he made the claim, noting that Jesus never actually says in Scripture, "I am God." However, if one enters the language and cultural assumptions of first-century Judaism, the claim is clear. In fact, Rabbi Neusner argues just this in his book *A Rabbi Talks with Jesus* on why he, as a good Jew, cannot accept Jesus. Not only did Jesus make this claim implicitly time and again by both words and mighty deeds but his divine actions also led him into confrontations that made him a threat, in both political and socio-economic terms, to those in power. Given the times, it is not surprising that Jesus met with death at the hands of the Romans and at the promptings of the religious authorities.

Not only did Jesus claim to be God but he also claimed to be the Messiah – again, often not directly, but implicitly through the cultural language of the people. Jewish prophecies from Moses to David to Isaiah to the minor prophets directed Israel's hopes toward a great figure whom God would send – a figure who later came to be called the 'Messiah', or 'Anointed One.' In Greek, the term is the 'Christ.' This figure would fulfill the prophetic, priestly, and kingly roles in Jewish society and make Israel a light to the nations.

By the time of Jesus, the Jews had lived under the yoke of foreign domination for centuries and had suffered many religious problems. They were therefore in great need of such a leader. David's united kingdom of Israel was split in 930 BC, after his death. Then the kingdom of Israel in the north fell to the Assyrians in 720 BC, and the kingdom of Judah in the south was crushed by the Babylonians in 586 BC. The Persians and then the Greeks took control of Palestine over the coming centuries, with only a brief period of independence, beginning in 140 BC, thanks to Judas Maccabaeus and his brothers. Then in 63 BC, Pompey ended this respite by conquering Palestine for the Roman Empire, bringing us into the times of Jesus.

At the time of Christ, the priestly, prophetic, and kingly offices in Jewish society were all in a dismal state. The sons of the despotic and illegitimate vassal-king Herod the Great sat on thrones over segments of Palestine, with Judea itself later being given directly to a Roman procurator because of the brutality of Herod Archelaeus. And, of course, all these rulers were subject to the Roman emperor, under whom the land was exploited of its resources, the provincials were crushed by taxes, and local political opponents were given the slave's penalty of crucifixion until death. This was the fate many of the other messiah-claimants met.

Jesus was not like other messiah-claimants. The goal of other messiah-claimants was to overthrow the Romans and claim the throne as the Maccabees had done more than a century before. A successful messiah-claimant had to survive, obviously, so that he could rule on that throne and bring justice to the people. Due to their political indiscretions and their combat losses in the face of the indomitable armies of Rome, none of them did survive. Much to the consternation of Jesus' disciples, survival was hardly even on his to-do list. Jesus knew that his destiny was to die and rise again. He spoke of his 'hour,' and he embraced and revealed his identity and purpose progressively. In his early life, Jesus did little to attract the critical eye of the authorities. During his early ministry, while causing some eyebrows to be raised among the authorities, he urged anyone who knew his messianic identity to maintain silence. Then, when he sensed his 'hour' was approaching, he revealed his identity and mission more openly and more provocatively, which led to his death.

After evoking from Peter and the other apostles a confession of faith in him as the Christ, Jesus began to reveal to them his approaching death and resurrection. On the first occasion, we are told, "Peter took him aside and began to rebuke him, 'God forbid, Lord! No such thing shall ever happen to you.' He turned and said to Peter, 'Get behind me, Satan! You are an obstacle to me. You are thinking not as God does, but as human beings do'" (Mt. 16:22-23). Not only was Jesus to meet this destiny but he would also actively pursue it. We read in the Gospel of Mark of Jesus' final ascent to Jerusalem: "They were on the way, going up to Jerusalem, and Jesus went ahead of them. They were amazed, and those who followed were afraid" (Mk. 10:32). At that point he gathered the apostles once more to tell them what would happen to him in Jerusalem. Yet even after this, they continued to think in terms of the usual messiah-script. James and John asked him, "Grant that in your glory we may sit one at your right and the other at your left" (Mk. 10:37). Jesus rebuked them, saying that glory in the Kingdom of God comes through humble service and suffering. He told them that the

Kingdom of God is not like the kingdoms of the world: "You know that those who are recognized as rulers over the Gentiles lord it over them, and their great ones make their authority over them felt. But it shall not be so among you. Rather, whoever wishes to be great among you will be your servant" (Mk. 10:42-43).

From a worldly perspective, Jesus does not fit the mold. He was a man of paradox. Christians profess him as fully human yet fully God. He was a king, yet born in a stable. He was a prophet who didn't mince words, yet he was meek and humble. He was punished for all human sin but was, himself, utterly sinless. A messiah-claimant, he was never a claimant to the throne, the offices of the Temple, or the established seats of teaching authority. Furthermore, despite being a messiah-claimant, he never wielded a sword, yet he was killed in the same manner as those who did.

This book is the second volume of *The Life and Times of Jesus,* a series that offers a popular history of Jesus. The series sheds light on, and supports historically, the Christ professed by faith. In the first volume, *The Life and Times of Jesus: From His Earthly Beginnings to the Sermon on the Mount,* we saw how Jesus fit into the society, history, and culture of the Jews of his time and saw how he emerged as an itinerant preacher, gathering disciples to himself and proclaiming the Kingdom of God in word and deed. We learned of the significance of the Temple and examined the politics of Palestine under Roman rule. Establishing Jesus' historicity from various sources, we saw how the canonical Gospels are nonetheless the most reliable account of Jesus' life.

In this second volume, *The Messiah behind Enemy Lines,* we will focus in a similarly historical manner on the provocative nature of Jesus' words and actions, which led to his sacrificial death on the cross and, in turn, to his resurrection. While this book builds on the cultural background laid out in the first volume, which hopefully you will take the opportunity to read, you can certainly start here as well. In this book, we will consider Jesus' human and supernatural enemies, the life of prayer that was the source of his action, and his hearers' response to him in both doubt and faith.

We will also journey with him through his transfiguration, his Last Supper and institution of the Eucharist, his betrayal and trial, and ultimately his passion, death, and resurrection, in light of the historical record. Finally, we will discuss his ascension, his sending of the Holy Spirit, and the apostles' developing understanding of their master's mission. But first, our journey will begin by considering Jesus' messianic identity, which he initially kept secret – under wraps until his 'hour' was close at hand.

Tensions from the Beginning

Each year, Jewish men all over Palestine would make a pilgrimage to Jerusalem to participate in the Passover, the celebration of God's liberation of their forefathers from slavery in Egypt. Each family, or groups of smaller families, would provide a lamb, which they could buy in the Temple's vast Court of the Gentiles, to be sacrificed on the altar. They would then eat the sacrificial lamb at their Passover meal, either in a room that they would rent for their family in Jerusalem or simply at a convenient spot in the surrounding fields. Vendors would set up booths and would often take advantage of the poor in their need for a perfectly unblemished animal to sacrifice, those being the only sacrifices that the priests would accept. Meanwhile, since only shekels were accepted for the Temple tax because of their higher silver purity (though the original reason was the idolatrous graven image on other coins), moneychangers would take Greek or Roman coins at a highly profitable rate of exchange. Furthermore, according to O'Reilly and Dugard, the Temple authorities would then take the collected money and loan it out to peasants with high interest; and when the poor could not repay the loans, the Temple authorities would repossess the peasants' homes, properties, and livelihood.

Like most Jewish men, Jesus too went down for the feast, with his disciples. According to John's Gospel, confrontation was manifest even during the first Passover of Jesus' public ministry. Jesus was moved to anger by the injustice committed at Jerusalem in God's name. We read, "He made a whip out of cords and drove them all out of the temple area, with the sheep and oxen, and spilled the coins of the money-changers and overturned their tables, and to those who sold doves he said, 'Take these out of here, and stop making my Father's house a marketplace'" (Jn. 2:15-16). Temple guards were likely stationed nearby, but they did not arrest Jesus. The Messiah was indeed to come to God's Temple and perform such an act. The prophet Malachi had foretold, "Now I am sending my messenger – he will prepare the way before me; and the lord whom you seek will come suddenly to his temple; the messenger of the covenant whom you desire. ... But who can endure the day of his coming? Who can stand firm when he appears? For he will be like a refiner's fire, like fuller's lye. He will sit refining and purifying silver, and he will purify the Levites [the priestly tribe], Refining them like gold or silver, that they may bring offerings to the LORD in righteousness" (Mal. 3:1-3). But was Jesus truly the Messiah? The religious authorities were fairly certain he was not, but they feared the crowds, many of whom did believe. So they began to watch Jesus closely for an opportunity to trip him up.

Not long afterward, when Nicodemus, a member of the Sanhedrin (the Jewish high court) who believed that Jesus was a prophet, wished to discourse with him, he could do so only at night out of fear of his fellow Pharisees. Jesus was a threat to the establishment. For one, he was not one of them. He did not belong to any of the existing parties of the Jewish leaders, nor was he educated by them. Jews of the ruling class typically belonged to either the Pharisees or the Sadducees and had to get along with their Roman overlords regardless of their antipathy for the latter.

The teachings of the Pharisees were popular among the middle and lower classes since the Pharisees stayed among the people and offered practical lessons. They believed that a strict practice of Moses' ceremonial law was essential to holiness, and they believed in the oral Torah – concerning further implications of how the laws were to be practiced – that Moses purportedly passed down. The Pharisees believed in an afterlife and in the resurrection of the body. They contributed greatly to the formation of Judaism as a religion, helping it to survive past the eventual destruction of the Temple (and, hence, the end of priestly cult) by focusing on rabbinic traditions of Torah interpretation and on living in ritual purity. Jesus harshly upbraided the Pharisees for their attitudes and their emphasis on minutiae over the heart of the Torah. While establishing a strong presence in Galilee, the Pharisees tended to think little of Galileans since many of the people there did not concern themselves with ritual purity; after all, the Temple – the place that required strict purity for worship – was far to the south. Many of the scribes, the Jewish learned men who fulfilled functions such as teacher, lawyer, judge, and scholar, were from among the Pharisees.

The Sadducees, on the other hand, accepted only the Torah, the first five books of the Bible, as Scripture, and rejected the traditions of the rabbis. Many modern scholars believe them to be associated with priestly families and the upper class. In Jesus' time, they held many positions of power, such as in the Sanhedrin. After the destruction of the Temple, the Sadducees, along with the priestly lines, vanished from the scene of Judaism since there was no longer a fitting place to offer the sacrifices that signified Israel's faithfulness to the covenant. They did not believe in an afterlife or the resurrection of the body. <u>The Sadducees were particularly hostile to Jesus, whom they may have particularly despised because of what they saw as his disregard for the Temple.</u>

There were other parties as well, though they did not hold many positions of power at the time of Christ. The Essenes set themselves apart from the religious life of the nation, practicing a life of strict asceticism in small communities. They believed they would please God through maintaining strict ritual purity. The Essenes rejected the worship in the Temple because they believed that the high priests were illegitimate in their lineage. Instead, they awaited the return of the last-presiding true high priest, whom they called the "Teacher of Righteousness." Meanwhile, the Zealots sought to overthrow the Romans through violence as Judas Maccabeus had done with the Greek Seleucids. The Zealots ultimately doomed the Temple by provoking the Romans through an uprising, which the Zealots started but behind which most all Jews rallied.

The Pharisees and the Sadducees had little reason to accept Jesus. As the comfortable establishment, they did not want trouble with the Romans at that time. Any messiah-claimant would greatly upset the delicate balance they sought to maintain. Jesus wasn't directly a military threat to either the Jewish authorities or the Romans, as other messiah-claimants often were. However, the religious authorities were afraid that if the people all rushed after him, they would cause a seditious disturbance, which the Romans would brutally crush. The Gospel of John reports the concerns voiced in the Sanhedrin in the days leading up to Christ's death: "What are we going to do? This man is performing many signs. If we leave him alone, all will believe in him, and the Romans will come and take away both our land and our nation" (Jn. 11:48). With the Temple having been recently and grandly renovated, they did not want to risk anything that could jeopardize its safety.

Furthermore, given his behavior at Passover, they saw Jesus as disrespectful of the Temple – and as upsetting the economics of the lucrative business that went on there. Importantly, they believed that Jesus was leading the people away from the proper practice of the Torah. According to the Talmud of the rabbis, Jesus "deceived and led Israel astray." The religious authorities saw him as disrespectful of the Sabbath and of the teachings of the rabbis. Biblical scholar N. T. Wright says of their viewpoint, "Jesus was following, and advocating, an agenda which involved setting aside some of the most central and cherished symbols of the Judaism of his day, and replacing them with loyalty to himself."

Jesus believed that the religious leaders were themselves the ones leading Israel astray. He denounced them, saying, "Oh Pharisees! Although you cleanse the outside of the cup and the dish, inside you are filled with plunder and evil. ... Woe to you Pharisees! You love the seats of honor in synagogues and greetings in marketplaces. Woe to you! You are like unseen graves over which people unknowingly walk" (Lk. 11:39, 43-44). The Pharisees instructed the people that one pleases God by following Moses' laws of ritual purity scrupulously. According to the Mosaic Law, the priests must cleanse themselves before entering the Temple. The Pharisees took this prescription a step further to require ritual purification before the Sabbath meal, at least for members of the Pharisee party, which then evolved into purification before meals in general. Jesus is saying in the Gospel of Luke that they have missed the point of the Law of Moses – internal purity of heart, which bodily purity only symbolizes. He had similar words for the scribes: "Woe also to you scholars of the law! You impose on people burdens hard to carry, but you yourselves do not lift one finger to touch them" (Lk. 11:46).

After the incident in the Temple, the people asked Jesus, "What sign can you show us for doing these things?" (Jn. 2:18). But no sign would truly suffice for the religious authorities. They actually did not question the supernatural character of Jesus' mighty deeds. They knew that he must be either of God or of Satan. But they would not even consider that he might be from God. That would have been too risky to their comfortable positions. The scribes accused, "By the prince of demons he drives out demons" (Mk. 3:22). The Talmud of the rabbis likewise claims he did this by "sorcery."

Jesus' battle, however, was not chiefly with the religious authorities. It was with the invisible forces of darkness that held the people in hostage and that had tempted the religious authorities to this hardness of heart. As Jesus said, "If a kingdom is divided against itself, that kingdom cannot stand" (Mk. 3:24). Essential to Jesus' mission of proclaiming the Kingdom of God was demolishing that of Satan, the fallen angel who set himself and his minions against the will of God.

Proclaiming Victory over Evil

We read of Jesus in the Gospel of John, "the light shines in the darkness, and the darkness has not overcome it" (Jn. 1:5). From the beginning, Jesus was a marked man, and the more he revealed himself, the more pointedly targeted he would become. As Jesus would explain to Nicodemus, "the light came into the world, but people preferred darkness to light, because their works were evil" (Jn. 3:19). The Gospel of Mark emphasizes Jesus' battles with the invisible forces of evil; the Gospel of John emphasizes his battles of words with the religious authorities. This was all leading up to the great battle at Christ's passion, of which he would say to those who arrested him, "this is your hour, the time for the power of darkness" (Lk. 22:53).

Jesus' mere presence gave him away. No sooner had he gathered his first disciples at Capernaum, on the north shore of the Sea of Galilee, than a demon in a possessed man cried out in the synagogue: "What have you to do with us, Jesus of Nazareth? Have you come to destroy us? I know who you are – the Holy One of God!" (Mk. 1:24). The demon revealed Jesus' identity, but Jesus did not accept its treacherous testimony. We read, "Jesus rebuked him and said, 'Quiet! Come out of him!' The unclean spirit convulsed him and with a loud cry came out of him. All were amazing and asked one another, 'What is this? ... He commands even the unclean spirits and they obey him.' His fame spread everywhere throughout the whole region of Galilee" (Mk. 1:25-28).

It is no wonder that when Jesus performed miracles or exorcisms, the Gospel of Mark records him as commanding those he healed to silence until the time was right for him to reveal himself more openly and thus to expose himself to greater danger. There was also another reason for what is called the 'messianic secret.' According to Scott Hahn and Curtis Mitch, "Jesus wanted to avoid a sensationalist reputation of being no more than a wonderworker. Publicizing his deeds by word of mouth comes with the danger that rumors will begin to disconnect his miracles from his saving message." Jesus wanted to reveal himself slowly through his words and actions in a way that inspired faith, not mere credulity.

We read in the Gospel of Mark that "he drove out many demons, not permitting them to speak because they knew him" (Mk. 1:34). While Jesus had an added reason for silencing the demons, it was a common practice in Jewish exorcisms to command them to silence. Words from the minions of Satan are malevolent and produce no good. In identifying Jesus, their possible motives may have been to express fear of him, to stir sensationalism among the people, or to expose Jesus to the authorities before his time.

Reference to demons and the Devil occurs throughout the Old and New Testaments. The Jews believed that demons sought to live in the bodies of humans or even animals. They also established specific prayers for exorcism, which often involved long incantations. Psalm 91 was often used as a prayer of exorcism. There we read, "You who dwell in the shelter of the Most High, who abide in the shade of the Almighty, Say to the LORD, 'My refuge and fortress, my God in whom I trust.' He will rescue you from the fowler's snare, from the destroying plague.... You shall not fear the terror of the night nor the arrow that flies by day" (Ps. 91:1-3, 5). What was unusual about Jesus' exorcisms was that he needed no special formulas, amulets, or ritual actions. He simply commanded, and the demons obeyed. The Jews, however, believed that it was possible for lesser demons to be cast out by more powerful demons. Therefore, the scribes, not believing in Jesus' divine origin, said of him, "He is possessed by Beelzebul." 'Beelzebul' means 'Lord of the Flies' and refers to Satan.

Jesus proclaimed the Kingdom of God not only by words but also by actions; thus, to discount the exorcisms of Jesus is to deny an important element of his proclamation of the Kingdom of God in action – his active demonstration of his victory over Satan. Yet some modern scholars dismiss the exorcisms of Jesus, noting that ancient peoples, including the ancient Jews, attributed nearly all diseases to these invisible, malevolent beings. Fr. James Martin writes in his book *Jesus: A Pilgrimage* of a balanced perspective on the matter: "Here's one way to think about it. First, some of the possessions in the Gospels seem rather to be the manifestation of physical illness. ... But there are some Gospel stories that still, two thousand years later, do not lend themselves so easily to scientific explanations – stories in which the demon is able to identify Jesus as the Messiah at a time when others around him (including his closest followers) still have no clue; stories in which the demons speak of themselves, oddly, in the plural, as when they identify themselves as 'legion'; stories in which the demons enable people to do frightening physical feats, such as bursting through chains." The Catholic Church still performs exorcisms. According to the *Catechism of the Catholic Church,* "When the Church asks publicly and authoritatively in the name of Jesus Christ that a person or object be protected against the power of the Evil One and withdrawn from his dominion, it is called *exorcism.* Jesus performed exorcisms and from him the Church has received the power and office of exorcizing" (no. 1673).

Pope Benedict XVI reflects in *Jesus of Nazareth* on the close of the Lord's Prayer, in which one prays, "but deliver us from evil." He explains that 'evil' is rightly translated in the singular and, as such, refers inseparably both to eternal loss and to the Devil who effects it. He writes, "the last petition brings us back to the first three: In asking to be liberated from the power of evil, we are ultimately asking for God's Kingdom, for union with his will, and for the sanctification of his name." Thus, deliverance from the Evil One is central to Jesus' mission of proclaiming the Kingdom.

Jesus said, "When an unclean spirit goes out of a person it roams through arid regions searching for rest but finds none. ... Then it goes and brings back with itself seven other spirits more evil than itself, and they move in and dwell there.... Thus it will be with this evil generation" (Mt. 12:43, 45). This passage follows immediately after Jesus' lament over the state of his own people. Thus, N. T. Wright says, "I think it highly unlikely that these verses are a sad commentary on the temporary nature of exorcisms. ... Rather, as Matthew's closing sentence [v. 45], and Luke's context, seems to indicate, this is a kind of *parable* about *Israel*. Here is the link between the exorcisms and the overall mission of Jesus ... the exorcisms themselves were signs that this god wished to deliver Israel herself from the real enemy who is now pitted against her: satan." Wright then proposes that the 'house' in the parable is the Temple and speculates on the nature of the 'exorcism': "If specific movements are in mind, we might perhaps think of the Maccabaean revolt, when 'the house' was 'swept and put in order'; or perhaps the Pharisaic movement as a whole, attempting to cleanse the body and soul of Judaism by its zeal for a purity which in some ways reflected that of the Temple; or possibly Herod's massive rebuilding programme, which produced a 'house' that was magnificent but in which (according to Jesus, and probably many of his contemporaries) YHWH [God] had no inclination to make his dwelling. ... Nothing short of a new inhabitation of 'the house' would do." This new habitation of God was eventually understood to be in the Church and in the hearts of the faithful. As St. Paul wrote, "Do you not know that you are the temple of God, and that the Spirit of God dwells in you?" (1 Cor. 3:16).

Israel was not the only nation in need of exorcism, by any means. The Gospel of Mark recounts how Jesus came upon a demoniac after crossing the Sea of Galilee to the Land of the Gerasenes in the Decapolis. Domesticated pigs, unclean animals according to the Jewish law, feature in the narrative, and they would only have been raised by Gentiles. Furthermore, the Gentiles likely worshipped pagan idols. Mark recalls, "When he got out of the boat, at once a man from the tombs who had an unclean spirit met him" (Mk. 5:1). The Gospels often refer to demons as 'unclean spirits.' The point of ritual cleanness was to symbolize holiness for God, so this spirit represented the opposite. Moreover, the tombs were, in the Jewish mind, an epitome of uncleanliness. "The man had been dwelling among the tombs, and no one could restrain him any longer, even with a chain. In fact, he had frequently been bound with shackles and chains, but the chains had been pulled apart by him and the shackles smashed, and no one was strong enough to subdue him. Night and day among the tombs and on the hillsides he was always crying out and bruising himself with stones" (Mk. 5:3-5). Jesus engaged the demon and commanded it to give its name, for calling someone by name was a demonstration of authority over that person, according to Jewish culture. Then he ordered the demon out of the man. The demon replied, "Legion is my name. There are many of us" (Mk. 5:9). Mark continues, "And he pleaded earnestly with him not to drive them away from that territory" (Mk. 5:10).

Hahn and Mitch offer an allegorical commentary based on the teachings of the Venerable Bede: "The demoniac represents the Gentile nations saved by Christ. As pagans, they once lived apart from God amid the tombs of dead works, while their sins were performed in service to demons. Through Christ, the pagans are at last cleansed and freed from Satan's domination." In the end, Jesus commanded the demon – or demons – to leave and allowed them to enter a herd of swine, which subsequently ran off a cliff into the sea and were drowned. Hence evil, often biblically portrayed as rising from the sea, was pushed back to its domain.

The Father and I Are One

In his book *A Rabbi Talks with Jesus*, Rabbi Jacob Neusner engages in serious dialogue with the teachings of Jesus on the Torah, the first five books of the Bible, and is impressed by many of his teachings and interpretations. But the key point of divergence for the rabbi is that Jesus placed himself at the center of his teaching in the place of God, the Torah, and the Temple. In the Sermon on the Mount, Jesus offered us a series of teachings in the following pattern: "You have heard that it was said to your ancestors... But I say to you..." (Mt. 5:21-22). He plumbed the depths of the commandments, teaching us to avoid not only murder but also anger, not only adultery but also lust, not only taking God's Name in vain but also all swearing. The rabbi points out that the reference to what "was said" is to the commands of God to Moses for all the people. Neusner writes, "Yes, I would have been astonished. Here is a Torah-teacher who says in his own name what the Torah says in God's name. ... I am troubled not so much by the message ... as I am by the messenger." The content of Jesus' teaching is not wholly other from the Torah; instead, he cut to the heart of it. For example, sayings in the Proverbs and the teachings of other rabbis occasionally reach interior depths of understanding that Jesus more fully plumbed.

Furthermore, Jesus taught on another occasion, "Whoever loves father or mother more than me is not worthy of me, and whoever loves son or daughter more than me is not worthy of me…" (Mt. 10:37). For Rabbi Neusner, this principle is not properly descriptive of the relationship between a rabbi and his disciples because it violates the command "Honor your father and your mother, that you may have a long life in the land the Lord your God is giving you" (Ex. 20:12). Neusner points out that "life in the land" means inclusion among the people God has gathered for himself and that no rabbi should interfere with this.

Moreover, Jesus not only breaks the Sabbath, which is the day that makes Israel what it is by entering God's rest, but he also argues in terms that replace the Temple with himself. In response to the accusation that he allowed his disciples to pick grain on the Sabbath because they were hungry, Jesus said, "Have you not read what David did when he and his companions were hungry, how he went into the house of God and ate the bread of offering, which neither he nor his companions but only the priests could lawfully eat? Or have you not read in the law that on the Sabbath the priests serving in the temple violate the Sabbath and are innocent? I say to you, something greater than the temple is here" (Mt. 12:3-6). Rabbi Neusner comments that "he can only mean that he and his disciples may do on the Sabbath what they do because they stand in the place of the priests in the Temple: the holy place has shifted, now being formed by the circle made up of the master and his disciples."

For Pope Benedict XVI in *Jesus of Nazareth*, such points underscore what Christians have always believed – that Jesus, the Messiah, is God incarnate. Jesus spoke in place of what God said in the Torah because he is the same God who said it. According to the *Catechism of the Catholic Church*, God's teaching in the Old Testament "involves a specific divine pedagogy: God communicates himself to man gradually" (no. 53). What is new here, too, is that his followers will live 'in' Christ and with the help of his

43

grace. For Pope Benedict, Jesus commanded that his disciples love him more than their parents because he is God. Furthermore, this meant that, in the new covenant, what constitutes membership in the Church no longer depends on a genealogy of flesh, as membership in the assembly did for Israel; rather, it depends on the transmission of God's Spirit. Finally, Jesus' explanation for allowing his disciples to break the Sabbath on the basis of precedents surrounding the Temple meant that he is the new Temple – the perfect dwelling place of God and the perfect place of sacrifice. His disciples assumed the place of priests because that was what they were in the Church that Jesus founded in fulfillment of the Israel of old.

In the Gospel of John, Jesus makes the claim to his divinity more directly. The scene is the Portico of Solomon, and the occasion is the Feast of the Dedication, now known as Hanukkah – the last one of his earthly life. Noticing Jesus there, a suspicious crowd, having seen his many signs and heard his many astonishing words, surrounds him and asks, "How long are you going to keep us in suspense? If you are the Messiah, tell us plainly" (Jn. 10:24). Jesus responds, "I told you and you do not believe. The works I do in my Father's name testify to me" (Jn. 10:25). Continuing his speech, Jesus closes with these words: "The Father and I are one" (Jn. 10:30). At that the people become incensed. According to Deuteronomy, "Anyone who blasphemes God shall bear the penalty," which was stoning (Deut. 24:15). So, John continues, "The Jews again picked up rocks to stone him. Jesus answered them, 'I have shown you many good works from my Father. For which of these are you trying to stone me?' The Jews answered him, 'We are not stoning you for a good work but for blasphemy. You, a man, are making yourself God'" (Jn. 10:31-33).

Interestingly, not all early believers accepted that Jesus was truly God. A Christian priest in Alexandria by the name of Arius (d. 336) was scandalized by the idea that God could become incarnate in a particular man. He taught that Jesus was a creature of God, but that he was the firstborn of all creatures. He said of the Son of God, "There was a time when he was not." This idea spread quickly throughout the Roman world. The emperor Constantine, who had recently legalized and then officially favored the Christian faith, called a council of bishops at Nicaea, in Asia Minor, in AD 325 to settle the matter because of the confusion it was causing. The council, analyzing the Christian Scriptures, condemned Arius' teachings and taught instead that the Son of God, who became incarnate in time, was coeternal with the Father but that the Father was his origin from all eternity. It declared that the Son is "one in being with the Father" – a statement that was later enshrined in the Nicene Creed, which is professed by Catholics and Protestants alike. For this reason, Pope Benedict writes that the most important thing Jesus has brought is not a particular insightful ethical teaching for humanity but, rather, this: "He has brought God."

Signs of God's Power

The writer of the Gospel of John arranges into the narrative seven 'signs' that Jesus performed to show that he was sent by God. They are reminiscent of the signs of Moses, who thereby showed his authority from God. We read in the book of Exodus, "But Moses said to God, 'Who am I that I should go to Pharaoh and bring the Israelites out of Egypt?' God answered: I will be with you; and this will be your sign that I send you. When you have brought the people out of Egypt, you will serve God at this mountain" (Ex. 3:11-12). The First Vatican Council spoke of the importance of signs in showing the reasonableness of faith in God's revelation, observing that "in order that the 'obedience' of our faith should be 'consonant with reason', God has willed that to the internal aids of the Holy Spirit there should be joined external proofs of His revelation, namely: divine facts, especially miracles and prophecies which, because they clearly show forth the omnipotence and infinite knowledge of God, are most certain signs of a divine revelation, and are suited to the intelligence of all" (*Dei Filius* no. 3).

Scholars commonly identify the first part of the Gospel of John after the Prologue as the 'Book of Signs.' First, Jesus changes water into wine at a wedding at Cana, at his mother's prompting and because of the embarrassment that running out of wine would cause the couple. Second, he heals a royal official's dying son; and third, he cures a paralytic. After a large crowd gathers to hear Jesus' teaching in a remote area, Jesus multiplies five loaves and two fishes to feed the multitude – his fourth sign. Fifth, as the disciples are fishing at night in a boat on the Sea of Galilee, Jesus approaches them, walking on the water. Sixth, Jesus encounters a man born blind and causes him to see. As his seventh sign in the Book of Signs, Jesus hears that his friend Lazarus is ill but does not go to him until after Lazarus has died. Jesus approaches the tomb, has the stone removed, and commands the dead man to arise and come out – and he does. This foreshadows Jesus' own resurrection, which takes place at the end of John's Gospel, and it is therefore the chief sign he offers.

Jesus did not want people merely to remain amused or enthralled by signs, yet he provided the signs to demonstrate the truth of his words. When Jesus returned to Cana in Galilee after celebrating the Passover in Jerusalem, a royal official approached him with a request to heal his dying son. Jesus replied, "Unless you people see signs and wonders, you will not believe" (Jn. 4:48). The man who approached Jesus was likely a Gentile courtier of Herod Antipas, who ruled in Galilee. We are told that the official's son lay ill in Capernaum, so it seems that he made an almost twenty-mile journey to make this request. We read, "The royal official said to him, 'Sir, come down before my child dies.' Jesus said to him, 'You may go; your son will live.' The man believed what Jesus said to him and left. While he was on his way back, his slaves met him and told him that his boy would live" (Jn. 49-51). Jesus required faith of the man and then granted his request. John continues, speaking of the royal official and his slaves, "He asked them when he began to recover. They told him, 'The fever left him yesterday, about one in the afternoon.' The father realized that just at that time Jesus had said to him, 'Your son will live,' and he and his whole household came to believe" (Jn. 4:52-53).

Not everyone understood the meaning of the signs. As Jesus went up a mountain near the shore of the Sea of Galilee, a large crowd of 5,000 men, not counting women and children, followed Jesus because they knew he was a miracle-worker. Jesus wanted to lead them beyond that. He cured some of their sick and then saw that they had come out to this remote area without bringing much food. Jesus wanted to lead his disciples, as well, to greater faith, so he asked Philip, "Where can we buy enough food for them to eat?" (Jn. 6:5). Philip's answer was much like ours – on an earthly level, anxious for what to do. Phillip replied, "Two hundred days' wages worth of food would not be enough for each of them to have a little [bit]" (Jn. 6:7). A young boy offered five barley loaves and two fishes, and Jesus' disciple Andrew brought them to the Master. Jesus had the disciples instruct the people to recline on the grassy mountainside in anticipation of being served a meal. The disciples were likely nervous since they did not have the food with which to provide for the people, and surely they would be ridiculed – or worse. We read in the Gospel, "Then Jesus took the loaves, gave thanks, and distributed them to those who were reclining, and also as much of the fish as they wanted. When they had had their fill, he said to his disciples, 'Gather the fragments left over, so that nothing will be wasted.' So they collected them, and filled twelve wicker baskets with fragments from the five barley loaves that had been more than they could eat" (Jn. 6:11-13).

Seeing the sign, the people believed that Jesus was the Messiah – but only on their terms and according to their worldly messiah-script. They still did not have unconditional faith in him, which Jesus said is a gift from God. We read, "Since Jesus knew that they were going to come and carry him off to make him king, he withdrew again to the mountain alone" (Jn. 6:15). For Jesus to be made into a political 'messiah' after their own liking would destroy his true mission; but the people did not give up. They were still there the next day, so Jesus went out to them to show them, by way of discourse, the true meaning of his sign of multiplying the loaves. He explained, "Amen, amen, I say to you, it was not Moses who gave the bread from heaven; my Father gives you the true bread from heaven. For the bread of God is that which comes down from heaven and gives life to the world" (Jn.

6:32-33). They found this acceptable, but Jesus continued, "I am the bread of life; whoever comes to me will never hunger, and whoever believes in me will never thirst" (Jn. 6:35). His words implied that he was greater than Moses, who had given the people manna from Heaven. According to the Talmud, written after the time of Christ but reflecting views of rabbis at that time, "None are like unto Moses." Furthermore, Jesus was like the people; he was from their own region, so how could he have come down from Heaven?

But Jesus pressed further: "Amen, amen, I say to you, unless you eat [*esthio*] the flesh of the Son of Man and drink his blood, you do not have life within you" (Jn. 6:53). Eating the flesh of a man and drinking his blood was not a symbol natural to the Jews, as Fr. Robert Barron points out. Cannibalism was prohibited by oral tradition, and there was even a prohibition in the Law of Moses against consuming blood, even naturally mixed in the meat from animals. The reason was that blood represented the life of the animal, and a human being must not take the life of a brute beast into himself. According to Deuteronomy, "But make sure that you do not eat of the blood; for blood is life" (Deut. 12:23). However, we must take into ourselves the life that Jesus has as God; the blood of the incarnate God in our veins is *essential* to our eternal life as children of God.

The people didn't like the analogy, but he didn't change it. He continued, "Whoever eats [*trogo*] my flesh and drinks my blood has eternal life, and I will raise him on the last day. For my flesh is true food and my blood is true drink" (Jn. 6:54-55). To the Jews, this would have been especially disturbing. Here the Gospel writer has Jesus switching to use of the Greek verb *trogein* to describe the eating of his flesh. Fr. Barron notes that this verb, which literally means to 'munch' or 'gnaw,' stresses the physicality of eating. Moreover, Jesus directly said that his flesh and blood are "true food" and "true drink." Later, in the account of the Last Supper, we read in language reminiscent of the multiplication of the loaves, "While they were eating, he took bread, said the blessing, broke it, and gave it to them, and said, 'Take it; this is my body.' And then he took a cup, gave thanks, and gave it to them, and they all drank from it. He said to them,

'This is my blood of the covenant, which will be shed for many'" (Mk. 14:22-24).

Even though the crowds had witnessed his multiplication of the loaves, they grumbled against what Jesus was now saying. They said, "This saying is hard; who can accept it?" (Jn. 6:60). Jesus often set a challenge before those who asked for his healing, in order to test their faith; he did not usually heal in the Gospels without first testing the person's faith. In a similar way, it seems that Jesus was here setting a stumbling block before the people, over which they needed to make a leap of faith. Many still do not, and he accepts that. Earlier in the discourse, Jesus had taught, "No one can come to me unless the Father who sent me draws him, and I will raise him on the last day" (Jn. 6:44). John continues, "As a result of this, many [of] his disciples returned to their former way of life and no longer accompanied him. Jesus then said to the Twelve, 'Do you also want to leave?'" (Jn. 6:66-67). Peter, who is often seen in the Gospels as the spokesmen of the Apostles, answered him, "Master, to whom shall we go? You have the words of eternal life.

We have come to believe and are convinced that you are the Holy One of God" (Jn. 6:68-69).

A Light to the Nations

The religious focus of the Jews as the Chosen People was with the nation of Israel as a people holy and set apart for the Lord. But the Hebrew Scriptures speak of the purpose of Israel's holiness – they were ultimately to be a light to the nations through witnessing to the presence of the God of all creation. God promised to Abraham, "in your descendants all the nations of the earth will find blessing" (Gen. 22:18). Also, we read in the book of the prophet Isaiah, "Arise! Shine, for your light has come, the glory of the Lord has dawned upon you. Though darkness covers the earth, and thick clouds, the peoples, upon you the Lord will dawn, and over you his glory will be seen. Nations shall walk by your light, kings by the radiance of your dawning" (Is. 60:1-3). Likewise, the Psalms speak of the Gentiles coming to worship the God of Israel: "Give to the Lord, you families of nations, give to the Lord the glory due his name! Bring gifts and enter his courts.... Tremble before him, all the earth; declare among the nations: The Lord is king" (Ps. 96:7-10).

According to the Second Vatican Council, "Christ is the Light of nations" (*Lumen Gentium* no. 1). Just before his ascension, Jesus said to his disciples, "All power in heaven and on earth has been given to me. Go, therefore, and make disciples of all nations, baptizing them in the name of the Father, and of the Son, and of the Holy Spirit, teaching them to observe all that I have commanded you" (Mt. 28:18-20). In fact, three of the four Gospels were written for a Gentile audience; only Matthew was intended primarily for Jews. However, as the Chosen People, the Jews were the first recipients of the Gospel message, with the focus shifting to the Gentiles after Jesus' resurrection.

In the Gospel of John, the approach of Gentiles to Jesus in faith signals to him the approach of his 'hour.' We read, "Now there were some Greeks among those who had come up to worship at the feast. They came to Philip ... and asked him, 'Sir, we would like to see Jesus.' Philip went and told Andrew; then Andrew and Philip went and told Jesus" (Jn. 12:20-22). Jesus' answer was surprising – a seeming digression. He replied, "The hour has come for the Son of Man to be glorified. Amen, amen, I say to you, unless a grain of wheat falls to the ground and dies, it remains just a grain of wheat, but if it dies, it produces much fruit. ... I am troubled now. Yet what should I say? Father, save me from this hour? But it was for this purpose that I came to this hour. Father, glorify your name" (Jn. 12:23-24, 27-28). Jesus' death was for the redemption of not only the Jews but also the whole world, and it would open the door of faith to the Gentiles.

The Gospel of Mark, likely written for the Christian community at Rome, presents several striking passages about Gentiles coming to faith in Christ. Jesus made an excursion to the district of Tyre in Syrian Phoenicia. A local Gentile woman believed that her daughter was possessed by a demon so, when she heard that Jesus was in town, she went to see him. His answer to her was this: "Let the children be fed first. For it is not right to take the food of the children and throw it to the dogs" (Mk. 7:27). 'Children' refers to the Children of Israel and 'dogs' was the term sometimes used by Jews to refer to Gentiles. He seemed to be implying that the time of ministry to the Gentiles had not yet come, but he was also challenging her to faith. Mark continues, "She replied and said to him, 'Lord, even the dogs under the table eat the children's scraps.' Then he said to her, 'For saying this, you may go. The demon has gone out of your daughter.' When the woman went home, she found the child lying in bed and the demon gone" (Mk. 7:28-30). Just after this, Jesus made another excursion into a Gentile territory – the region of the Decapolis, to the east of the Sea of Galilee. There he healed a deaf man with a speech impediment, and the people had much faith in him. Mark tells us of the locals, "They were exceedingly astonished and they said, 'He has done all things well. He makes the deaf hear and the mute speak'" (Mk. 7:37).

In the Gospel of Luke, a God-fearing Roman centurion sent Jewish elders to Jesus while at Capernaum to ask him to heal his slave. This man, though he was a Gentile, was a believer in the God of Israel and even a major benefactor of the local synagogue. Jesus went with the elders, but before he arrived at the house, the centurion sent men to Jesus with this message: "Lord, do not trouble yourself, for I am not worthy to have you enter under my roof. Therefore, I did not consider myself worthy to come to you; but say the word and let my servant be healed. For I too am a person subject to authority, with soldiers subject to me. And I say to one, 'Go,' and he goes; and to another 'Come here,' and he comes; and to my slave, 'Do this,' and he does it" (Lk. 7:6-8). So Jesus healed his servant from afar, and for saying this, this Gentile warrior received Jesus' highest compliment in the Gospels: "I tell you, not even in Israel have I found such faith" (Lk. 7:9).

Through Jesus, and particularly by his death and resurrection, the Gentiles were drawn into fellowship with the God of Abraham, Isaac, and Jacob. Thus, the Gospel of Mark, which seeks to answer the question of Jesus' identity, places the final answer in the mouth of another Roman centurion – the one standing at the foot of the cross. Astonished at the manner of Jesus' death, he confesses, "Truly this man was the Son of God!" (Mk. 15:39).

The Lord's Prayer: Our Father in Heaven

Jesus was a man of prayer. St. Thomas Aquinas teaches that Jesus had the full vision of God even while on earth. One can only imagine Jesus going off by himself early in the morning to pray, as he does frequently in the Gospels. Focusing on this vision in silence, he would thank the Father for his good gifts, intercede for those around him, and find himself renewed in his human understanding of the will of God.

Jesus' disciples greatly admired his prayer and wished to emulate it. Once after he returned from prayer, Luke tells us, they asked of him, "Lord, teach us to pray just as John taught his disciples" (Lk. 10: 1). Jesus responded with what we call the Lord's Prayer. The familiar version of the prayer comes from Matthew's Gospel:

> Our Father who art in heaven,
> Hallowed be thy name.
> Thy kingdom come.
> Thy will be done,
>   On earth as it is in heaven.
> Give us this day our daily bread;

> And forgive us our trespasses,
>> As we forgive those who trespass against us;
>> And lead us not into temptation,
>> But deliver us from evil (Mt. 6:9-13 [RSV-CE]).

St. Thomas Aquinas writes in his *Catechetical Instructions*, "Among all other prayers, the Lord's Prayer holds the chief place." Jesus primarily meant this as an example of how to pray. Pope Benedict writes in *Jesus of Nazareth*, "the words of the Our Father are signposts to interior prayer, they provide a basic direction for our being and they aim to configure us to the image of the Son. The meaning of the Our Father goes much further than the mere provision of a prayer text. It aims to form our being, to train us in the inner attitude of Jesus."

Today, people often speak of God in a general way as 'Father' since he is the Creator of human beings and has a special relationship with them. But the Old Testament does not call God 'Father' very often. On one of those few occasions, it refers to the future son of David saying, "I will be a father to him, and he shall be a son to me" (2 Sam 7:14). While immediately referring to Solomon, Christians take this verse as ultimately referring to Christ. A Father has the same nature as his child. If the man Christ uniquely possessed the divine nature, then only he was the 'Son of God' in the full sense of the term. After Christ's coming, however, St. Paul wrote in his Letter to the Romans, "For those who are led by the Spirit of God are children of God. ... [And] you received a spirit of adoption, through which we cry, '*Abba*, Father!'" (Rom. 8:14-15). Now followers of Christ call God their Father since Jesus has invited them and because they share in God's nature through their 'adoption,' which his great love makes possible. Still, only Jesus says "my Father." For Christians, it is only in communion with all other believers that we call God "our Father." Christians thereby recognize fellow believers as their own brothers and sisters in Christ.

Our Father 'in Heaven' distinguishes God from our earthly fathers. While some people may have difficulty with God as 'Father' because of their image of their particular earthly father, Pope Benedict writes that God "is the measure and source of all fatherhood," not the other way around. Pope Benedict further notes that while the Old Testament often uses maternal imagery and symbolism for God's nurturing love, it never calls him "Mother." He writes, "The mother-deities that completely surrounded the people of Israel and the New Testament Church ... imply some form of pantheism in which the difference between Creator and creature disappears. ... By contrast, the image of the Father was and is apt for expressing the otherness of Creator and creature and the sovereignty of his creative act." Furthermore, "the prayer language of the entire Bible remains normative for us."

There are seven petitions in all that Jesus gives in the version of the prayer found in Matthew's Gospel. Pope Benedict writes, "Three are 'thou-petitions,' while four are 'we-petitions.' The first three petitions concern the cause of God himself in this world; the four following petitions concern our hopes, needs, and hardships. The relationship between the two sets of petitions in the Our Father could be compared to the relationship between the two tablets of the Decalogue. Essentially, they are explications of the two parts of the great commandment to love God and

67

our neighbor – in other words, they are directions toward the path of love." According to St. Thomas Aquinas, the Lord's Prayer teaches us that "our prayer ought to be ordered as our desires should be ordered." Thus, it is fitting that the first three petitions concern God. As Jesus taught, "seek first the kingdom [of God] and his righteousness, and all these things will be given you besides" (Mt. 6:33).

The first petition is "Hallowed be thy name." When God appeared to Moses in the Burning Bush, Moses asked God for his name to give to the people. God's answer was, "I am who I am" (Ex. 3:14). He would not be constrained by a particular name, since a name, in their culture, would place him under the power of the person who called and would imply being on the same plane as the other gods. Therefore, the Israelites honored this name of God, spelled with the Hebrew consonants YHWH (Yahweh), and were forbidden by the post-exilic tradition of the rabbis to utter the name out loud, much less to take this name "in vain," as forbidden by the Ten Commandments (Ex. 20:7). The high priest would only pronounce the name of God, YHWH, once a year in the Holy of Holies of the

Temple on the Day of Atonement. In fact, so guarded was utterance of the name of God that to this day some scholars hold that the original pronunciation of YHWH is not certain. All this care pointed to the proper disposition we ought to have for God (awe for his holy transcendence. In this spirit, the Psalmist prays, "O LORD, our Lord, how awesome is your name throughout all the earth!" (Ps. 8:2). According to Pope Benedict, the meaning of Christ's first petition in the Lord's Prayer is "that he [God] himself take charge of the sanctification of his name, protect the wonderful mystery of his accessibility to us, and constantly assert his true identity as opposed to our distortion of it."

The second petition is "Thy kingdom come." God's Kingdom refers to his domain, in which all things are subject to him. St. Thomas Aquinas writes, "a king sometimes has only the right to a kingdom or dominion, and yet his rule has not been declared because the men in his kingdom are not as yet subject to him. His rule or dominion will come only when the men of his kingdom are his subjects." While God is the Creator of all and rules all things by his providence,

69

Jesus taught that the Kingdom of God is like a mustard seed, which "springs up and becomes the largest of plants" (Mk. 4:32).

This is closely related to the next petition: "Thy will be done, on earth as it is in heaven." Pope Benedict says of Jesus, "his oneness with the Father's will is the foundation of his life. The unity of his will with the Father's will is the core of his very being." For Christians, conscience helps one discern the will of God, which includes following his commandments. Pope Benedict teaches that 'heaven' refers to where God's will is done perfectly, and he identifies Jesus himself with heaven. Sin and evil, which are opposed to God's will here on earth, will exist no more in Heaven, since the Book of Revelation says that "nothing unclean will enter it" (Rev. 21:27).

Thus, with the first three petitions, Jesus is teaching us that these dispositions toward God are prerequisite for whatever else we may ask for.

The Lord's Prayer: Give Us This Day

Sometimes people only pray when they need something. Jesus teaches by the example of the Lord's Prayer that prayer should be not only about our need, but also about God's glory. Pope Benedict writes, "If man is to petition God in the right way, he must stand in the truth. And the truth is: first God, first his Kingdom. The first thing we must do is step outside ourselves and open ourselves to God." God recognizes our needs and is waiting to give us what we require. Pope Benedict writes that this is "what prayer is really all about: It is not about this or that, but about God's desire to offer us the gift of himself – that is the gift of all gifts, the 'one thing necessary.' Prayer is a way of gradually purifying and correcting our wishes and of slowly coming to realize what we really need: God and his Spirit."

Now we come to the set of petitions that Jesus has his followers ask for themselves. The fourth petition of the Lord's Prayer asks, "Give us this day our daily bread." Pope Benedict points out that Jesus here refers to the poverty of his disciples and the call of all his followers to poverty of spirit, which entails reliance on God rather than on the security of material things. Jesus taught, "So do not worry, and say, 'What are we to eat?' or 'What are we to drink?' or 'What are we to wear?' All these things the pagans seek. Your Heavenly Father knows you need them all" (Mt. 6:31-32). For St. Thomas Aquinas, asking for our 'daily bread' also guards against excess and greed. Pope Benedict further teaches that in asking for our daily bread, Jesus reminds us to pray for the needs of others as well.

For the Church Fathers, 'daily bread' had another spiritual meaning. Origen, an early Church Father, pointed out that the Greek word translated here as 'daily' (*epiousios*) was extremely rare – perhaps even invented by the Gospel writer for a special and unique purpose. St. Jerome translated it in Latin as *supersubstantialis* – 'super-substantial.' He had in mind that as God provided manna from Heaven for the hungry Israelites in the desert, he supernaturally nourishes us with Jesus, the Bread of Life. According to St. Thomas Aquinas, this spiritual meaning is twofold – referring to both the Eucharist and the Word of God. He writes, "in the first meaning, we pray for our Sacramental Bread which is consecrated daily in the Church, so that we receive it in the Sacrament, and thus it profits us unto salvation. ... In the second meaning this bread is the Word of God: 'Not in bread alone doth man live, but in every word that proceedeth from the mouth of God.'" Pope Benedict writes that, in fact, "the Fathers of the Church were practically unanimous in understanding the fourth petition of the Our Father as a eucharistic petition."

The fifth petition is "And forgive us our trespasses, as we forgive those who trespass against us." The word for 'trespasses' is often translated as 'debts,' and the imagery may be that of the debts of the poor, which were supposed to be dissolved every seven years during the Jubilee year. Forgiveness is a major theme of the Gospels. For St. Thomas, the first part of this petition requires Christians to acknowledge humbly that they have offended God and to have sorrow for sin, and it leads to hope in God's forgiveness and promise of salvation. In the second part of the petition, Jesus links our forgiveness by God with our forgiveness of those who have done us wrong. It is reminiscent of the Parable of the Unforgiving Servant, in which Jesus tells of a servant who was forgiven a large debt by his master but then refused to forgive a small debt to his fellow servant. Pope Benedict writes, "Whatever we have to forgive one another is trivial in comparison with the goodness of God, who forgives us." Jesus teaches that forgiveness is the answer to those who cause evil, thus ending the cycle of violence.

7

In this seventh petition is prayed "lead us not into temptation." The word here for temptation implies a test rather than a seduction; Jesus does not mean that God literally tempts people to sin but, rather, that he permits this to happen so that good may come of it. In fact, Jesus often tested the faith of those who asked for healing, and many of those people found healing and grew in their faith. Pope Benedict quotes St. Paul, who says, "God is faithful, and he will not let you be tempted beyond your strength, but with the temptation will also provide the way of escape, that you may be able to endure it" (1 Cor. 10:13 [RSV-CE]). But Jesus instructs his followers here to pray that God not submit them to this; hence, some Bible translations render 'temptation' in this instance as 'the final test' (NABRE). Pope Benedict writes out the meaning of this petition in his own words: "I know that I need trials so that my nature can be purified. When you decide to send me these trials, when you give evil some room to maneuver, as you did with Job, then please remember that my strength goes only so far. Don't overestimate my capacity. Don't set too wide the boundaries within which I may be tempted, and be close to me with your protecting hand when it becomes too much for me."

Next we come to the final petition: "But deliver us from evil." Christians believe that Jesus came for this purpose – for redemption and, thus, deliverance from evil. Jesus, the redeemer and exorcist, is seen as the ultimate warrior against the Evil One who has gained great dominion over humanity. According to Pope Benedict, 'evil' here can also be translated 'Evil One,' and he teaches that these two are closely connected. Furthermore, he warns that we should not be concerned only with such evils as the loss of this or that but, first and foremost, with the loss of our soul due to the temptations of the Devil. Therefore, Pope Benedict writes, "the last petition brings us back to the first three: In asking to be liberated from the power of evil, we are ultimately asking for God's Kingdom, for union with his will, and for the sanctification of his name." If Christ has conquered sin and evil, then to him belongs the victory.

The final doxology, often prayed by Protestants at the end of the Lord's Prayer, praises God for this victory over evil: "For thine is the kingdom, and the power, and the glory, now and forever." The Reformers added this to the Lord's Prayer based on an old manuscript of the Gospel of Matthew, which included it at the end of the prayer. As modern critical scholarship shows, the doxology was added into that manuscript years after Jesus taught his disciples how to pray. The editor of the manuscript, in turn, had copied it from the liturgy, in which it was placed after the Lord's Prayer. However, a similar prayer is found in the Old Testament. The aged King David praised the Lord as offerings came forward for the building of the Temple, which was to be accomplished under his son Solomon: "Yours, Lord, are greatness and might, majesty, victory, and splendor" (1 Chron. 29:11). Today, Catholics pray the doxology at Mass, after the Lord's Prayer but separate from it.

The Crowds and the Believers

One of Jesus' chief pastoral concerns was to engender faith in the people, in his followers, and in those he healed. For Jews, faith meant faithfulness to the covenant between God and the people of Israel. Now Jesus required faith in him – a loyalty that included belief in Jesus as the central hope of the promises of the covenant. The question of who Jesus is pervades the earlier chapters of the Gospel of Mark. After Jesus calms the storm on the Sea of Galilee, Mark says of the disciples in the boat, "They were filled with great awe and said to one another, 'Who then is this whom even the wind and sea obey?'" (Mk. 4:41). The answer comes later on, when we read that "he asked his disciples, 'Who do people say that I am?' They said in reply, 'John the Baptist, others Elijah, still others one of the prophets.' And he asked them, 'But who do you say that I am?' Peter said to him in reply, 'You are the Messiah.' Then he warned them not to tell anyone about him" (Mk. 8:27-30).

Jesus' focus was on the poor, the sick, the disenfranchised, and sinners. In the Gospel of Luke we read, "The Pharisees and their scribes complained to his disciples, 'Why do you eat and drink with tax collectors and sinners?' Jesus said to them, 'Those who are healthy do not need a physician, but the sick do. I have not come to call the righteous to repentance but sinners'" (Lk. 5:30-32). Tax collectors were regarded as 'sinners' both because of their extortion for personal profit beyond what was required and for their loyalty to the government, which was seen as opposed to the true aspirations of the people. Other 'sinners' likely included prostitutes. N. T. Wright teaches that 'repentance' for Jews means turning oneself around so as to return to the covenant. He further says that it was an expectation that the Messiah would bring the people back to the covenant and that Jesus' outreach to 'sinners' is symbolic of the return of the people to God. Thus, Jesus began his ministry saying, according to the Gospel of Mark, "This is the time of fulfillment. The kingdom of God is at hand. Repent, and believe in the gospel" (Mk. 1:15).

For Rabbi Neusner, one of the most troubling things about Jesus is that his demands and aims were not primarily for the whole nation of Israel but for those who were loyal to him. The rabbi writes that even when Jesus did address 'Israel' as a whole, "the Israel here is not family and village ... if what should concern me is his kingdom and his righteousness, where I live, with whom I live – these really bear no consequence. ... This 'Israel' is then something other than, different from, that Israel of home and family that I know." Two issues are therefore salient here for the rabbi – the first being that Jesus' message was disconnected from the community and the second being that Jesus' 'Israel' was not identical with the old Israel.

The first charge, however, is simply not the case since even the earliest of Christian life was a communal life. Even if some churches today preach an individualist message, this was foreign to Jesus. As Jesus identified the covenant with himself, he likewise identified his followers with himself. When he approached Saul on the latter's way to persecuting Christians in Damascus, Jesus appeared to him and asked, "why are you persecuting me?" (Acts 9:4). However, regarding the rabbi's second objection, it is true that Jesus did not win over – or even attempt to win over – the whole nation of Israel with its temporal power structures.

Biblical scholar N. T. Wright asks, "But did Jesus intend to bring the whole of Israel – say, all Jews living in Galilee and Judea in the 20s AD – into his following? Was he aiming to mount a renewal movement that would sweep the board, propelling him into a position of undisputed national leadership? All the indications are to the contrary. That is not how the kingdom was to come, according to parables, like the sower." St. Paul wrote to Gentile Christians at Rome, "Indeed you will say, 'Branches were broken off so that I might be grafted in.' That is so. They were broken off because of unbelief, but you are there because of faith. ... a hardening has come upon Israel in part, until the full number of the Gentiles comes in, and thus all Israel will be saved" (Rom. 11:19-20, 25-26). This, presumably, has not happened yet.

The earliest of Christians, believing themselves to be the New Israel, formed close-knit communities. We read of the Christians in the Acts of the Apostles, "They devoted themselves to the teaching of the apostles and to the communal life, to the breaking of the bread and to the prayers. ... All who believed were together and had all things in common; they would sell their property and possessions and divide them among all according to each one's need. Every day they devoted themselves to meeting together in the temple area and to breaking bread in their homes. They ate their meals with exultation and sincerity of heart, praising God and enjoying favor with all the people. And every day the Lord added to their number those who were being saved" (Acts 2:42-47).

N. T. Wright proposes that the fellowship of believers began even before Jesus' resurrection. He points out that while Jesus called many to faith in him, he did not ask everyone to follow him in his journey of preaching and ministry. Examples of the latter include Jesus' friends in Bethany – Martha, Mary, and Lazarus. Wright compares the fellowship of the early believers back at home with the fellowship of the Essenes, the Pharisees, the followers of John the Baptist, and other groups within Judaism. He says that believers during Jesus' own lifetime, in addition to attending synagogue with their fellow villagers, would have been united already in prayer (praying to

God as 'Father'), belief (Jesus as Messiah), and practice (living out the teachings of the Sermon on the Mount).

No doubt, Jesus was popular among the common people. In the Gospel of Mark we read, "Hearing what he was doing, a large number of people came to him also from Jerusalem, from Idumea, from beyond the Jordan, and from the neighborhood of Tyre and Sidon" (Mk. 3:8). Given that Jesus was in Capernaum at the time, this means that people came on foot from great distances to see him. For example, Tyre was about 30 miles away, Jerusalem 80 miles, and Idumea 120 miles. Jesus was, in fact, so popular that the Gospels often show him withdrawing from the crowds to pray and asking people not to spread the word about where he was staying the night. Fr. James Martin writes, "When considering Jesus' enormous appeal, we might recall the disciples who immediately abandoned their old lives to follow him, the grateful men and women he had cured of illnesses, the delighted parents of healed children, the forgiven sinners turned into followers, and the great crowds who followed him from town to town, who hung on his every word – and on his person too. Frequently people simply wanted to *touch* Jesus."

Rejection and Unbelief

Jesus also experienced much rejection, perhaps the most painful of which was from the jealousy of his own family and friends at Nazareth. The Gospel of Luke includes the rejection of Nazareth as one of the first events of Jesus' ministry. At the synagogue, Jesus got up, read from the scroll, and spoke about it. This in itself was not unusual since no one was exclusively designated to preach at the synagogues; it was the right of any devout adult Jewish male. We read, "He stood up to read and was handed a scroll of the prophet Isaiah. He unrolled the scroll and found the passage where it was written: 'The Spirit of the Lord is upon me, because he has anointed me to bring glad tidings to the poor. He has sent me to proclaim liberty to captives and recovery of sight to the blind, to let the oppressed go free, and to proclaim a year acceptable to the Lord'" (Lk. 4:16-19). This passage was often seen as a prophesy of the coming Messiah. Luke continues, "Rolling up the scroll, he handed it back to the attendant and sat down, and the eyes of all in the synagogue looked intently at him. He said to the listeners, 'Today this scripture passage is fulfilled in your hearing'" (Lk. 4:20-21).

This was too much for them – it was a claim to messiahship from a simple man whom they had watched grow up, who lacked special rabbinic training, and who had worked as a carpenter. Their reaction was incredulous: "They also asked, 'Isn't this the son of Joseph?' Jesus responded by testing their faith: 'Surely you will quote me this proverb, "Physician, cure yourself," and say, "Do here in your native place the things that we heard were done in Capernaum." ... Amen, I say to you, no prophet is accepted in his own native place'" (Lk. 4:23-24). Jesus went further, recalling times when God gave his grace to Gentiles when his own Chosen People were lacking in faith. As much as the people may have seen good in Jesus growing up, however, they had now had enough. Luke continues, "When the people in the synagogue heard this, they were all filled with fury. They rose up, drove him out of the town, and led him to the brow of the hill on which their town had been built, to hurl him down headlong. But he passed through the midst of them and went away" (Lk. 4:28-30).

The Gospel of Mark and the Gospel of Matthew also tell of a rejection of Jesus at the synagogue at Nazareth, although they record it later in his ministry. These narratives bear textual similarities to Luke's account while lacking the account of the townspeople's attempt to stone Jesus. Either this was the same event or, perhaps, Jesus returned to Nazareth a second time only to be rejected again. Both Matthew and Mark point out that Jesus was not able to work wonders at Nazareth because of the people's lack of faith, since faith was a prerequisite for healing. Mark tells us, "So he was not able to perform any mighty deed there, apart from curing a few sick people by laying his hands on them. He was amazed at their lack of faith" (Mk. 6:5-6).

The Pharisees' and Sadducees' rejection of Jesus prompted many other Jews, as well, to reject Jesus. Rabbi Neusner, speaking primarily of evangelization efforts by early Christians after Jesus' earthly life, says, "Wherever the rabbis' views of Scripture were propagated the Christian view of the meaning of biblical, especially prophetic, revelation and its fulfillment made relatively little progress." Even in

Christ's time this was so. Jesus was less popular in Jerusalem and Judea, which were more under the influence of the religious leaders. Also, since the Judeans were close to the Temple and, hence, typically followed stricter purity codes, they tended to look down upon Galileans, such as Jesus, who were generally known for their more lenient religious practices.

Therefore, in the Gospel of John, we see a great deal of conflict waiting for Jesus in Jerusalem and in Judea. At Jesus' final and triumphant entry into Jerusalem, he was hailed with Davidic royal slogans and greeted with people waving palm branches in hand, as for a king. However, this crowd comprised not locals but, for the most part, the people from various regions who had followed him thus far. In fact, the Gospel of Matthew recounts that "when he entered Jerusalem the whole city was shaken and asked, 'Who is this?' And the crowds replied, 'This is Jesus the prophet, from Nazareth in Galilee'" (Mt. 21:10-11). We read also, in the Gospel of John, that some synagogue leaders were already expelling those who believed in Jesus. In the account of Jesus' healing of a blind man at Jerusalem, we find that the blind man's parents are afraid to admit that it might have been Jesus who healed their son. We read, "His parents ... were afraid of the Jews, for the Jews had already agreed that if anyone acknowledged him as the Messiah, he would be expelled from the synagogue" (Jn. 9:22). The blind man openly confessed his faith in Jesus before the religious authorities, and they "threw him out" (Lk. 9:34).

Those concerned with the temporal affairs of Palestine had little interest in following Jesus. From Mark's Gospel we learn that Herod Antipas was afraid of Jesus. Herod said of Jesus, "It is John whom I beheaded. He has been raised from the dead" (Mk. 6:16). Furthermore, the Zealots, who wanted to overthrow the Romans, would have been dismayed at Jesus. According to N. T. Wright, "Anyone announcing the kingdom *but explicitly opposing armed resistance* was engaging in doubly serious political action: not only the occupying forces, but all those who gave allegiance to the resistance movement, would be enraged." Jesus was not concerned with this. As Simeon had prophesied of him as an infant in the

Temple, "Behold, this child is destined for the fall and rise of many in Israel, and to be a sign that will be contradicted" (Lk. 2:34).

The Approaching Hour

There were a number of times when Jesus was seemingly on the brink of either being stoned or arrested but, as the Gospel of John explains, "his hour had not yet come" (Jn. 7:30). Yet he knew his 'hour' of suffering and death was approaching, and the days for keeping his messianic identity a secret were numbered. Having demonstrated unique authority through powerful words and actions over the course of his ministry, he asked his disciples, "Who do people say that I am?" (Mk. 8:27). We read in the Gospel of Mark, "They said in reply, 'John the Baptist, others Elijah, still others one of the prophets.' And he asked them, 'But who do you say that I am?' Peter said to him in reply, 'You are the Messiah'" (Mk. 8:28-29). Having received and accepted this answer, Jesus went on to qualify what it meant to be the Messiah. We read, "He began to teach them that the Son of Man must suffer greatly and be rejected by the elders, the chief priests, and the scribes, and be killed, and rise after three days. He spoke this openly" (Mk. 8:31-33).

Jesus often called himself the 'Son of Man,' using the name in all four Gospels. As Hahn and Mitch point out, the phrase is used over a hundred times in the Old

Testament – usually meaning little more than 'human one' or 'mortal one,' but used in the Book of Daniel to describe a glorious figure who may be understood as the Messiah. The context is a dream Daniel had, in which he saw four beasts representing four empires that would dominate the land of Israel before the coming of God's redemption. After the four beasts came a glorious and righteous figure, to whom their dominion would give way. The prophet Daniel wrote, "As the visions during the night continued, I saw One like a son of man coming, on the clouds of heaven; When he reached the Ancient One and was presented before him, He received dominion, glory, and kingship; nations and peoples of every language serve him. His dominion is an everlasting dominion that shall not be taken away, his kingship shall not be destroyed" (Dan. 7:13-14). Sure enough, when finally asked at his trial before the Sanhedrin if he was the Messiah, Jesus answered, "I am; and 'you will see the Son of Man seated at the right hand of the Power and coming with the clouds of heaven'" (Mk. 14:62).

According to Hahn and Mitch, Jesus invoked both Old Testament meanings of 'Son of Man' at various points

– sometimes using the name to emphasize his solidarity with all of his fellow humans and other times to emphasize his identity with the messianic figure in the Book of Daniel. Here and throughout the latter part of the Gospel of Mark, as Jesus begins to tell his disciples about his coming suffering and death, he seems to be alluding to both senses – not only that, like any human, he too can suffer and die but also that such is the destiny of the Messiah. The idea that the Messiah could suffer and die was astonishing for the disciples, as for any first-century Jews; the Messiah, they thought, could not perish. He had to save the people, not fall victim to the same plights as they did. According to Matthew's account of the same event, Peter spoke up saying, "God forbid, Lord! No such thing shall ever happen to you" (Mt. 16:22). But Jesus answered, "Get behind me, Satan! You are an obstacle to me. You are thinking not as God does, but as human beings do" (Mt. 16:23). This rebuke hearkened to the prophecy in Isaiah, "For my thoughts are not your thoughts, nor are your ways my ways, says the Lord. As high as the heavens are above the earth, so high are my ways above your ways and my thoughts above your thoughts" (Is. 55:8-9).

Jesus further told his disciples that they, too, needed to be ready to accept suffering for the Kingdom: "Whoever wishes to come after me must deny himself, take up his cross, and follow me" (Mk. 8:24). As first-century Jews, the disciples would have expected as much. The followers of the Messiah had to be ready to do battle and perhaps even die the death of a revolutionary at Roman hands – namely, crucifixion. But while this may have been what the disciples were thinking when Jesus spoke these words, the first readers of the Gospel of Mark at Rome would have known what Jesus was really talking about and taken comfort in it.

Scholars believe that the Gospel of Mark was written for the Christian community at Rome before AD 70. In AD 64, a great part of the city of Rome was destroyed by fire. The population found out that the culprit was the mentally disturbed Emperor Nero. Nero therefore placed the blame for the fire on the Christians and began fiercely hunting down and persecuting them. The Roman historian Tacitus wrote, "Yet no human effort, no princely largess nor offerings to the gods could make that infamous rumor disappear that Nero had somehow ordered the fire. Therefore, in order to abolish that rumor, Nero falsely accused and executed with the most exquisite punishments those people called Christians, who were infamous for their abominations. ... And perishing they were additionally made into sports: they were killed by dogs by having the hides of beasts attached to them, or they were nailed to crosses or set aflame, and, when the daylight passed away, they were used as nighttime lamps. Nero gave his own gardens for this spectacle and performed a Circus game, in the habit of a charioteer mixing with the plebs or driving about the race-course."

Jesus concluded his words on persecution and the 'cruciformity' of his followers in this way: "Amen, I say to you, there are some standing here who will not taste death until they see that the kingdom of God has come in power" (Mk. 9:1). In all three Synoptic Gospels (Matthew, Mark, and Luke), the transfiguration of Jesus immediately follows Jesus' first prediction of his passion and his call for his disciples to follow him in his suffering. Jesus' transfiguration was an event in which his glory was revealed clearly to Peter, James, and John. In the following chapter, we will see more on the meaning of this development.

The Transfiguration

After having explained to his disciples the evils that would befall him, Jesus then showed his core disciples the glory that was to come through that suffering so they would not be discouraged. We read in the Gospel of Mark, "After six days, Jesus took Peter, James, and John and led them up a high mountain apart by themselves. And he was transfigured before them, and his clothes became dazzling while, such as no fuller could bleach them" (Mk. 9:2-3). The Gospels do not tell us the name of the mountain, but tradition identifies it as Mt. Tabor in southern Galilee – a mountain with a glorious view of the patchwork farmland of the region. In the Bible, going up a mountain signifies prayer, so Pope Benedict tells us that this event gives us a glimpse of Jesus' prayer life. Jesus' heavenly nature was revealed as he appeared in a dazzling white garment. Mark continues, "Then Elijah appeared to them along with Moses, and they were conversing with Jesus" (Mk. 9:4). Moses represents the Law and Elijah the prophets, affirming Jesus' messianic fulfillment of their missions.

Awestruck, Peter spoke up: "Rabbi, it is good that we are here! Let us make three tents: one for you, one for

Moses, and one for Elijah" (Mk. 9:5). This is often seen as another obtuse and random response from Peter, and the Gospel does tell us "he hardly knew what to say" (Mk. 9:6), but Peter may have had more perception here than we give him credit for. The tents here refer to the *sukkoth*, translated as tabernacles or booths, which the Jews would build for the feast of Tabernacles to remind themselves of God's care for them during their wandering in the desert. The feast of Tabernacles, which takes place at the time of the final harvest in September or October, was celebrated in Palestine for seven days. Moses instituted the festival, as recorded in the Book of Exodus. The walls of the booths could be constructed from any material, but the roof had to be made from organic materials. Males slept in the booths each day during the festival, and all meals were eaten there.

Pope Benedict, citing the theologian Jean Danielou, S. J., points out that the booths not only reminded the Jews of how God had once cared for them in the desert but also of how he would provide a marvelous dwelling for them in the future time of the Messiah. In fact, Jesus used the word that refers to these tabernacles when he said, "I tell you, make friends for yourselves with dishonest wealth, so that when it fails, you will be welcomed into eternal dwellings" (Lk. 16:9). So perhaps Peter, having just confessed Jesus as the Messiah a few days earlier, likewise connected the appearance of Moses and Elijah to Jesus' messianic identity by offering to build the tents. Still it wasn't quite the right answer. God's answer came thundering from above. We read in Mark's Gospel, "Then a cloud came, casting a shadow over them; then from the cloud came a voice, 'This is my beloved Son. Listen to him'" (Mk. 9:7). The future tabernacle was in fact Christ; according to the Gospel of John, Jesus identified the Temple, the dwelling place of God, with himself (Jn. 2:19-21).

The transfiguration of Jesus exhibited a number of similarities to Moses' theophany experience at Mt. Sinai. While Moses went up Mt. Sinai to speak with God and receive the Ten Commandments, Jesus went up Mt. Tabor to be transfigured in prayer. We read of Moses, "As Moses came down from Mount Sinai with the two tablets of the commandments in his hands, he did not know that the skin of his face had become radiant while he conversed with the LORD" (Ex. 34:29). Likewise, Jesus changed in appearance gloriously and shone brilliantly. The Lord appeared to Moses in a cloud and pronounced his name to Moses. We read in the book of Exodus, "Having come down in a cloud, the LORD stood with him there and proclaimed his name, 'LORD'" (Ex. 34:5). Likewise, at the transfiguration, a cloud came over them and a voice proclaimed, "This is my beloved Son. Listen to him" (Mk. 9:7). No commandments were declared on Mt. Tabor, but the Word of God was proclaimed: "Listen to him." Moreover, while Moses was leading the people in exodus from Egypt toward the Promised Land, Jesus was beginning the New Exodus from the slavery of sin to eternal life with God.

Moses and Elijah likewise appear together in the prophecy in the book of Malachi that refers to the coming of the Messiah: "Remember the law of Moses my servant, which I enjoined upon him on Horeb, the statutes and ordinances for all Israel. Lo, I will send you Elijah the prophet, Before the day of the LORD comes, the great and terrible day to turn the hearts of the fathers to their children, and the hearts of the children to their fathers" (Mal. 3:23). On the way down the mountain, Jesus answered the disciples' questions about the prophecy that Elijah would come again before the Messiah. This was likely the prophecy in question. The mission of the prophet Elijah was to restore the people to God, so Jesus told his disciples that John the Baptist was the one who came in the spirit of Elijah to prepare the way for his coming.

Jesus would tell his disciples twice more about his coming passion and death in Jerusalem, and each time they would continue to be puzzled over it. What startled them even more was how he pressed on toward Jerusalem despite his prediction. We read, "They were on the way, going up to Jerusalem, and Jesus walked ahead of them. They were amazed and those who followed were afraid. Taking the Twelve aside again he began to tell them what was going to happen to him: 'Behold, we are going up to Jerusalem, and the Son of Man will be handed over to the chief priests and the scribes, and they will condemn him to death and hand him over to the Gentiles who will mock him, spit on him, scourge him, and put him to death, but after three days he will rise'" (Mk. 10:32-34).

The disciples were still perplexed about this. As Hahn and Mitch point out, while many Jews believed in the general resurrection of the dead at the end of the world, the disciples had no concept for the coming resurrection of Jesus or what it meant. All James and John could think about was the coming of messianic kingly glory. So they asked Jesus, "Grant that in your glory we may sit one at your right and the other at your left" (Mk. 10:37). Jesus responded with a lesson on the true meaning of greatness in the Kingdom of God: "You know that those who are recognized as rulers over the Gentiles lord it over them, and their great ones make their authority over them felt. But it shall not be so among you. Rather, whoever wishes to be great among you will be your servant; whoever wishes to be first among you will be the slave of all" (Mk. 10:42-44). Thus Jesus inverted the structures of power in the Kingdom of God – an ideal that the institutional Church tries to model, submitting itself to reform to this end since the worldly structures of powers always try to seep in. Then Jesus concluded saying, "For the Son of Man did not come to be served but to serve and to give his life as a ransom for many" (Mk. 10:45).

Jesus Enters Jerusalem

A few months after his transfiguration, at the time of the first harvest in the spring, Jesus made his last pilgrimage to Jerusalem for the Passover, knowing that he himself was the Passover Lamb to be sacrificed. But first he passed through Jericho, where a blind man named Bartimaeus called out to him. The man kept crying out, "Jesus, son of David, have pity on me" (Mk. 10:47). This was a title of the Messiah, and we read in the following verse that "many rebuked him." While perhaps they thought Bartimaeus was a bother, some of them may also have known that Jesus usually did not want to be called the Messiah openly and that doing so would be politically dangerous. But the time of the messianic secret was over; the time had come for Jesus to be "lifted up." Jesus called for the man and healed him of his blindness, saying, "Go your way; your faith has saved you" (Mk. 10:52). Mark then tells us that Bartimaeus immediately followed Jesus "on the way." Given that the name 'Bartimaeus' was still recorded in the writing of the Gospel decades after the fact, Richard Baukham suggests in *Jesus and the Eyewitnesses*, perhaps the man became part of the community of early

Christians, continuing to tell of how Jesus had healed him.

After this, Jesus and his followers trekked uphill to the outskirts of Jerusalem. They would have arrived at the Mount of Olives, with a view of Herod's Temple rising over the massive walls of the city across the Kiddron Valley. N. T. Wright tells us in *Mark for Everyone*, "If you've ever been to the Holy Land, you will know that to go from Jericho to Jerusalem involves a long, hard climb. Jericho is the lowest city on earth, over 800 feet below sea level. Jerusalem, which is only a dozen or so miles away, is nearly 3,000 feet above sea level. The road goes through hot, dry desert all the way to the top of the Mount of Olives, at which point, quite suddenly, you have at the same time the first real vegetation and the first, glorious sight of Jerusalem itself. ... Now add to that sense of excitement the feeling that Jewish pilgrims, coming south from Galilee, would have every time they went up to Jerusalem for a festival (as they did several times a year). They were coming to the place where the living God had chosen to place his name and his presence; the place where, through the regular daily sacrifices, he assured Israel of forgiveness, of fellowship with himself, of hope for their future."

Before entering the city, Jesus had two disciples bring him a colt that he prophesied they would find in the village. He mounted the colt and entered the city. We read, "Many people spread their cloaks on the road, and others spread leafy branches that they had cut from the fields. Those preceding him as well as those following kept crying out: 'Hosanna! Blessed is he who comes in the name of the Lord! Blessed is the kingdom of our father David that is to come! Hosanna in the highest!'" (Mk. 11:8-10). 'Hosanna' is an invocation meaning 'grant salvation,' but it is left untranslated to retain its original fullness. According to N. T. Wright, "'Hosanna' is a Hebrew word which mixes exuberant praise to God with the prayer that God will save his people, and do so right away." The people took their slogans from Psalm 118. There it is written of King David, "Lord, grant salvation [*hosanna*]! Lord, grant good fortune! Blessed is he who comes in the name of the Lord. We bless you from the Lord's house. The Lord is God and has given us light. Join in procession with leafy branches up to the horns of the altar" (Ps. 118:25-27).

All four Gospels record Jesus' triumphal entry into Jerusalem. Only John specifically mentions palm branches by name, recounting that "they took palm branches and went out to meet him" (Jn. 12:13), while Matthew and Mark say that they laid branches before him. Matthew, with his sights on Jewish Christians, sees the event as fulfilling a prophecy in Zechariah: "Rejoice heartily, O daughter Zion, shout for joy, O daughter Jerusalem! See, your king shall come to you, a just savior is he, meek and riding on an ass, on a colt, the foal of an ass" (Zech. 9:9). Luke tells us, "Some of the Pharisees in the crowd said to him, 'Teacher, rebuke your disciples.' He said in reply, 'I tell you, if they keep silent, the stones will cry out!'" (Lk. 19:39-40). Certainly, this kind of entry was dangerous because of the Romans.

Matthew's account gives us an idea of who these people were, who were declaring Jesus King of Israel. We read, "And when he entered Jerusalem the whole city was shaken and asked, 'Who is this?' And the crowds replied, 'This is Jesus the prophet, from Nazareth in Galilee'" (Mt. 21:10-11). Thus, it was not primarily the locals who greeted him (since there was a general prejudice in Judea toward Galileans) but, rather, the crowds that had followed him from both near and far. It was because of such people that the Sanhedrin sought to arrest Jesus at night and away from the crowds. Most likely, these were not the same people who would call for crucifixion at his trial before Pilate. Instead, the people who had celebrated his entry likely scattered out of fear at the news of Jesus' later arrest.

Therefore, it makes sense that even after being welcomed as King of Israel, Jesus lamented over the city: "Jerusalem, Jerusalem, you who kill the prophets and stone those sent to you, how many times I yearned to gather your children together, as a hen gathers her young under her wings, but you were unwilling!" (Mt. 23:37). Then he prophesied the destruction of the Temple, which would occur in AD 70 at the hands of the Romans. Upon hearing his disciples marvel at the grandeur of the Temple, he said, "You see all these things, do you not? Amen, I say to you, there will not be left here a stone upon another stone that will not be thrown down" (Mt. 24:2).

The Synoptic Gospels (Matthew, Mark, and Luke) place Jesus' cleansing of the Temple at this point while John, who alone mentions that Jesus "made a whip out of cords" to scatter the money-changers and vendors, places a similar event at the beginning of Jesus' ministry, during the first of the three Passovers. It is possible that only one event is being referenced and that the various Gospel writers placed it within their respective narratives based on theological reasons. Possibly, too, Jesus cleansed the Temple on two occasions; both timings offer historical plausibility. In John's account, Jesus is told that the Temple took 46 years to build (Jn. 2:20) – a number that separates the ministry of Jesus neatly from a key date in Josephus' record for the beginning of Herod's renovation project. On the other hand, the Synoptic account of the event, taking place on Jesus' last days in Jerusalem, provides particular motivation for the religious authorities to arrest Jesus and have him put to death, even though the event was not mentioned as an explicit accusation in any accounts of the trial.

The Last Supper

We read in the Gospel of John, "Before the feast of the Passover, Jesus knew that his hour had come to pass from this world to the Father. He loved his own in the world and he loved them to the end" (Jn. 13:1). The Passover was a great Jewish feast that celebrated and reenacted God's powerful redemption through liberation from slavery in Egypt. God sent Moses to Pharaoh with the message "Let my people go, that they may celebrate a feast to me in the desert," but the ruler refused (Ex. 5:1). So God sent terrible plagues on the land of Egypt, symbolic of the overthrow of their gods. Pharaoh still refused after nine plagues, so God sent a tenth plague – the death of the firstborn of every family of man and beast. This plague was directed against the heir to the 'immortal' Pharaoh's throne. But God told Moses to gather the Hebrew people and give them instructions on what to do so that God would pass over them, saving their firstborn: "This month shall stand at the head of your calendar; you shall reckon it the first month of the year. Tell the whole community of Israel: on the tenth of this month [Nisan] everyone one of your families must procure for itself a lamb, one apiece for each household. If a family is too small for a whole lamb, it shall join the nearest household. ... The lamb must be a year-old male and without blemish. You may take it from either the sheep or the goats. You shall keep it until the fourteenth day of this month, and then, with the whole assembly of Israel present, it shall be slaughtered during the evening twilight. They shall take some of its blood and apply it to the two doorposts and the lintel of every house in which they partake of the lamb. That same night they shall eat its roasted flesh with unleavened bread and bitter herbs. It shall not be eaten raw or boiled, but roasted whole, with its head and shanks and inner organs. None of it must be kept beyond the next morning; whatever is left over in the morning shall be burned up. This is how you are to eat it: with your loins girt, sandals on your feet and your staff in hand, you shall eat like those who are in flight. It is the Passover of the LORD. For on this same night I will go through Egypt, striking down every first-born of the land, both man and beast, and executing judgment on all the gods of Egypt – I, the LORD! But the blood will mark the houses where you are. Seeing the blood, I will pass over you; thus, when I strike the land of Egypt, no destructive blow will come upon you" (Ex. 12:2-13).

The Synoptic Gospels tell us that Jesus' Last Supper was a Passover meal. While John does not say it was a Passover meal, the features of the meal he describes suggest that it may have been. For John, what is important is that Jesus died at the same time the Passover lambs were being sacrificed in the Temple, thus showing him to be the true Passover lamb. According to Exodus, this was to be the fourteenth day of the month of Nisan (Ex. 12:6). John writes of the trial before Pilate, "It was preparation day for Passover, and it was about noon" (Jn. 19:14). The Passover lasted seven days, and the Passover Seder meal was to be celebrated on the first day – the day after the lambs were sacrificed in preparation. For John, Jesus' Last Supper had to be earlier than the first day of Passover, yet the Synoptic Gospels have Jesus' Last Supper as a Passover Seder meal. There are a number of theories to explain this. Certain theories reconcile the two accounts in light of varying known methods among first-century Jewish sects for calculating the Passover, much as the date of Easter is calculated differently by Christians of the West and those of the East. Thus, according to one calendar,

Jesus' Last Supper might have been on the first day of Passover while his death could have been on the preparation day for Passover according to a different calendar.

The Gospel of John devotes five chapters to Jesus' lessons, discourses, and prayers at the Last Supper. John's account begins with Jesus washing the feet of his disciples – an act that would typically have been performed by servants for the host's dinner guests because of the dusty roads in Palestine. Jesus says, "Do you realize what I have done for you? You call me 'teacher' and 'master,' and rightly so, for indeed I am. If I, therefore, the master and teacher, have washed your feet, you ought to wash one another's feet. I have given you a model to follow, so that as I have done for you, you also should do" (Jn. 13:12-15). In this, Jesus may be giving a demonstration of the humble service he provides for his followers through his death, and likewise modeling the humble service that his followers should offer others. It was one of the many times Jesus used his example of table-fellowship to teach his followers how they should live.

Jesus then gave them a commandment: "I give you a new commandment: love one another" (Jn. 13:34). The command to love was not itself new; it was written in the book of Leviticus, "You shall love your neighbor as yourself" (Lev. 19:18). According to Hahn and Mitch, "The Torah commanded *human* love for ourselves and our neighbor. Jesus commands *divine* love for one another that is modeled on his own acts of charity and generosity." Therefore, Jesus continues, "As I have loved you, so you also should love one another" (Jn. 13:34). Such love comes from God's grace in Christ. "I am the true vine, and my Father is the vine grower. ... Remain in me, as I remain in you. Just as a branch cannot bear fruit on its own unless it remains on the vine, so neither can you unless you remain in me" (Jn. 15:1, 3).

As Scott Hahn points out, what the Romans did to Jesus on the cross was not a sacrifice in the eyes of most passers-by but an execution of an unfortunate prophet and revolutionary. What made it a sacrifice was what Jesus did at the Last Supper. It was also the culmination of his many lessons for his disciples from table-fellowship. Thus, the Synoptic Gospels

(Matthew, Mark, and Luke) and St. Paul's First Letter to the Corinthians recall Jesus' self-offering through the institution of the Eucharist at the Last Supper.

If the meal was a Passover Seder, there was a strict order and protocol for such meals, as detailed in the Mishnah. Four cups of wine were to be offered, each with its own blessing. Scripture scholar Brant Pitre tells us in *Jesus and the Jewish Roots of the Eucharist* that the first cup involved wine mixed with a little water and would be offered with the blessing, "Blessed are you, O Lord, our God, King of the universe, who creates the fruit of the vine." After a light preliminary course is served, the second cup would be offered. The youngest boy would then ask the father, "Why is this night different from all other nights?" And the father would respond with the scriptural story of God's deliverance. Then a third cup would be prepared and a blessing given over the unleavened bread: "Blessed are you, O Lord our God, who brings forth bread from the earth." After the main meal was eaten, the third cup, called the cup of blessing, would be drunk. Finally, at the concluding rites, the fourth cup would be drunk, and the Hallel

Psalms (Ps. 115-118) would be sung in praise of God's deliverance. Hallel is a cognate of *hallelujah*, an invocation of praise for God, who mightily saves. At the Last Supper, Jesus altered this strictly prescribed rite. We read in the Gospel of Luke, "Then he took a cup, gave thanks, and said, 'Take this and share it among yourselves; for I tell you [that] from this time on I shall not drink of the fruit of the vine until the kingdom of God comes.' Then he took the bread, said the blessing, broke it, and gave it to them, saying, 'This is my body, which will be given for you; do this in memory of me.' And likewise the cup after they had eaten, saying, 'This cup is the new covenant in my blood, which will be shed for you'" (Lk. 22:15-20). Notice that two cups are mentioned here. Based on this account and on the tradition of the Seder meal, Pitre believes that the institution of the Eucharist took place at the third cup – the cup of blessing.

There is no mention of the fourth cup. Pitre believes that this, along with Jesus' statement that he will not drink from the cup again until the Kingdom comes, indicates that the common wine Jesus drank on the cross was actually the final cup of the Passover meal.

We read in the Gospel of John, "After this, aware that everything was now finished, in order that the scripture might be fulfilled, Jesus said, 'I thirst.' There was a vessel filled with common wine. So they put a sponge soaked in wine on a sprig of hyssop and put it up to his mouth. When Jesus had taken the wine, he said, 'It is finished.' And bowing his head, he handed over the spirit" (Jn. 19:28-30). The branch of the hyssop herb was the type that was used to sprinkle the blood of the Passover lamb on the doors of the Hebrews; it was also used for the sprinkling of blood at the Temple. Thus, the presence here of hyssop brings to mind images of Passover and sacrifice.

With a new covenant comes a new ritual to institute and perpetuate it. And Jesus spoke of a "new covenant in my blood" (Lk. 22:20). As the Hebrews were required to eat the whole lamb on the night of the Passover and the participants of the Seder meal were required to drink all four cups of wine completely, Jesus commanded his disciples to eat of his body and drink of his blood, and to "do this in memory of me." For the Jews, memory is not merely cognitive but entails participation through reliving an event of the past, making it present for a new generation.

Jesus Is Arrested

Immediately after the Last Supper, Matthew recounts, "Then Jesus went with them to a place called Gethsemani" (Mt. 26:36). 'Gethsemani' literally means 'oil press.' It was on the Mount of Olives and faced Jerusalem and the Temple Mount. The Garden of Gethsemani was known for the production of olive oil from its many large, gnarled olive trees. In fact, the garden has been preserved to the present day. In the evening twilight, on their way from the Upper Room on the outskirts of the city to the Mount of Olives, Jesus and his disciples would have passed a sweeping view of Jerusalem and the Temple Mount. The disciples sang the Hallel Psalms as they went on their way, since these were part of the Seder ritual. One such psalm is as follows: "In danger I called on the LORD; the LORD answered me and set me free. The LORD is with me; I am not afraid; what can mortals do against me? The LORD is with me as my helper; I shall look in triumph on my foes" (Ps. 118:5-8). They also would have sung, "Blessed is he who comes in the name of the LORD" (Ps. 118:26).

When they arrived at the garden – which brings to mind the image of the Garden of Eden, from which sin first arose – Jesus became distressed, and he asked the disciples to watch and pray since he knew that his 'hour' of suffering had arrived. He called Peter, James, and John – the same disciples to whom he had revealed his glory at his transfiguration and whom he had gathered at other important occasions – to be with him in his distress while the others remained a few yards behind. Jesus was burdened with severe mental stress in anticipation of the fearsome suffering ahead of him, because of the attacks of Satan and because the sins of the world came pressing down on him at this point. Satan, working through the darker tendencies of men to envy, greed, hatred, thirst for power, and thirst for blood, was much at work behind the evil and barbaric events that were unfolding and brought the brunt of his forces against Jesus. Further, Pope Benedict writes of Christ in *Jesus of Nazareth: Part II*, "Because he is the Son, he sees with total clarity the whole foul flood of evil, all the power of lies and pride, all the wiles and cruelty of the evil that masks itself as life yet constantly serves to destroy, debase, and crush life. Because he is the Son, he experiences deeply all the horror, filth, and baseness that he must drink from the 'chalice' prepared for him: the vast power of sin and death. All this he must take into himself, so that it can be disarmed and defeated in him."

Luke's Gospel tells us, "He was in such agony and he prayed so fervently that his sweat became like drops of blood falling on the ground" (Lk. 22:44). As Pope Benedict says, with his human will Jesus wished that there could be a way the suffering would pass, but with his divine will he desired the salvation of the world be accomplished in this most fitting way. He said, "Abba, Father, all things are possible to you. Take this cup away from me, but not what I will but what you will" (Mk. 14:36). Ultimately, he submitted his human will fully to the divine will and embraced the suffering ahead. Meanwhile, through all of this, Peter, James, and John had fallen asleep, perhaps because of the long day of Passover-related excitement and the four cups of wine they were each required to drink at the Seder meal. Jesus said to him, "Are you still sleeping and taking your rest? It is enough. The hour has come. Behold, the Son of Man is to be handed over to sinners. Get up, let us go. See, my betrayer is at hand" (Mk. 14:41-42).

The Sanhedrin had already met and decided that they needed to do away with Jesus at last. We read in the Gospel of John, "So the chief priests and the Pharisees convened the Sanhedrin and said, 'What are we going to do? This man is performing many signs. If we leave him alone, all will believe in him, and the Romans will come and take away both our land and our nation'" (Jn. 11:47-48). Caiaphas, the high priest, responded in an unwitting prophesy, "You know nothing, nor do you consider that it is better for you that one man should die instead of the people, so that the whole nation may not perish" (Jn. 11:49-50). While not everyone believed in Jesus, there were a sufficient number who held him in high regard – especially since so many people from Galilee were in town for the Passover festival – that the religious authorities feared what might happen if they tried to arrest him publicly. It was likely that a riot would break out, the Romans would intervene, and this would bring about exactly what the Sanhedrin feared from Jesus – the destruction of the nation and the Temple by the Romans, as would ultimately happen in AD 70. This is why Judas Iscariot, Jesus' traitorous disciple, was so valuable to them. He told them Jesus' private travel plans so that they could arrest him at night and without much incident. They offered Judas thirty pieces of silver for his services, which was a sum equivalent to 120 days' wages. This was prophesied in Zechariah: "Shepherd the flock to be slaughtered. ... And they counted out my wages, thirty pieces of silver" (Zech. 11:4, 12).

We read in the Gospel of Mark, "Then, while he was still speaking, Judas, one of the Twelve, arrived, accompanied by a crowd with swords and clubs who had come from the chief priests, the scribes, and the elders" (Mk. 14:43). In Luke's Gospel we read that "chief priests and temple guards and elders" came for the arrest. Who were these people? The Sanhedrin is seen in the Gospels as being composed of chief priests, scribes, and elders. While the Sanhedrin was always seen as a powerful Jewish assembly, there are scant and conflicting ancient sources on what the Sanhedrin really was, and its powers and scope waxed and waned for several hundred years both before and after Jesus. It seems the Sanhedrin, based at Jerusalem, was the highest court of the Jews, comprising 71 members including the high priest who presided over it, and it dealt with issues that were both religious and political. Members seemingly sat in a semicircle with two scribes standing in the middle – one to record the evidence against the accused and the other to record the evidence in favor of the accused. During the time of Jesus, the Sanhedrin did not have the authority to exact the death penalty since the Romans had taken that right away from them. Sometimes, however, they carried out the death penalty in between Roman procurators in Judea.

There was only to be a single high priest at the Temple; he was to be of the proper lineage, from among the line of Aaron, and was to serve for life. After murdering the Hasmonean royal-high-priestly line, Herod the Great appointed high priests at his own political pleasure or for payment for single-year terms, withholding from them much of the high priests' former temporal authority. After Herod's time, high priests were again appointed for indefinite terms; however, the Romans in effect deposed them at will. Former high priests probably became what the Gospels term as 'chief priests,' and they were likely aligned with the Sadducees. Scribes were scholarly men, well versed in the Law of Moses, who filled a number of functions in Jewish society including that of lawyer, teacher, and preacher, and many were of the party of the Pharisees. Elders were likely eminent laymen and priests who held membership within in the Sanhedrin, though sometimes the term refers in the Gospels to members of the Sanhedrin in general.

The Gospels tell us that Peter pulled out his sword and struck the ear of the high priest's servant. Luke tells us that Jesus miraculously restored the ear and healed the man. Thus, many in the crowd that came against Jesus in the garden were not professional soldiers but simply well-armed free men and slaves, who were sent by the members of the Sanhedrin for backup in case of trouble. The Temple guard, from whose ranks the soldiers likely came, was composed of Levites. Their primary duty was to stand watch at the gates of the Temple, keeping order and adding to the dignity of God's house; they were not a particularly powerful force.

According to the Synoptic Gospels, Jesus was bound and led away to the house of Caiaphas, the high priest, and the whole Sanhedrin gathered there for the event. Today pilgrims can visit the small dungeon at Caiaphas' house into which Jesus was likely lowered during his ordeal when not standing before the assembly. John tells us that Jesus was first brought to the house of Annas before being sent to Caiaphas. Annas was a former high priest whom many believed to be the rightful high priest since the Romans had wrongfully deposed him. Matthew's Gospel tells us that, at Caiaphas' house, false witnesses were brought before the whole assembly to accuse Jesus. By Jewish law, however, it was illegal for the Sanhedrin to decide capital cases at night. Matthew and Luke both tell us that the Sanhedrin convened the following morning to finalize their decision. Still, scholars doubt that what took place here was a real trial since the sessions lacked the due procedures for a capital case of the Sanhedrin. Since the Sanhedrin was barred at the time from condemning anyone to death, the final outcome of the session was simply to bring Jesus to capital trial before Pilate in order to do away with him.

As the charges were being laid before Jesus at night, the disciples made themselves scarce. Only Peter followed behind on the way to Caiaphas' house to see what was going to happen and where Jesus was going to be taken. But then Peter was discovered, leading to his threefold denial of even knowing the rabbi he had followed for three years and confessed to be the Messiah.

Meanwhile, the first false witness twisted Jesus' words and quoted him as saying, "I will destroy this temple made with hands and within three days I will build another not made with hands" (Mk. 14:58). Such a saying might be akin to someone today threatening to destroy the capitol. He would be regarded as a terrorist. In Jesus' day, he also would have been considered as one who profaned the Temple. Still, this testimony was not enough; and, as Mark tells us, "their testimony did not agree" (Mk. 14:59). Not mentioned are Jesus' cleansing of the Temple and his triumphal entry to Jerusalem, but we can be sure that these acts were on everyone's mind. These deeds were essentially claims to messiahship, so the high priest asked Jesus directly, "Are you the Messiah, the son of the Blessed One?" (Mk. 14:61). Scholars believe this account to be historically accurate because Jews, and most certainly the religious authorities, carefully avoided uttering the name of God. Instead of denial, like that of Peter, who was allowed to get away, Jesus gave an answer that he knew would lead to his death: "I am; and 'you will see the Son of Man seated at the right hand of the Power and coming with the clouds of heaven'" (Mk. 14:62). He identified the messianic prophecy of Daniel with himself and claimed a unique supernatural status of union with God. Though the high priest was forbidden by law to tear his garments, as was customary for those mourning or performing penance, we read, "At that the high priest tore his garments and said, 'What further need have we of witnesses?'" (Mk. 16:63). According to the Venerable Bede, this action signaled the end of the high priesthood of the old order.

The Trial of Jesus

We read, "Then the whole assembly of them arose and brought him before Pilate" (Lk. 23:1). This may have taken place the following morning, after his arrest. John tells us that Pilate was at the praetorium but that he had to come outside to the people since entering the house of a Gentile would render the Jews unclean for the Passover the following day. A 'praetorium' can be either a permanent building or a tent in a Roman military encampment that serves as a command post. The praetorium in Jerusalem might have been at the Fortress Antonia, which is the traditional starting point of the *Via Dolorosa* for pilgrims tracing the way of the cross, or – perhaps more likely – at the palace in Jerusalem that had been constructed by Herod the Great.

In 1961, archaeologists found an inscription at an amphitheater in Caesarea Maritima that mentions Pontius Pilate as 'prefect,' a position he held over the former domain of Herod Archelaeus. 'Procurator' was a later title given for the same position. Caesarea Maritima, on the coast of the Mediterranean and far from the heart of Jewish religion, was actually Pilate's headquarters, but he was in Jerusalem at the time to ensure order during the Passover. Pilate was born in Italy and was probably not particularly pleased to be made prefect of this distant region, though at least it was something to appease his thirst for power. He ruled the region surrounding Jerusalem directly by way of the army since the last client ruler, the ethnarch Herod Archelaeus, had been deposed by Rome decades before for his cruelty. Pilate, who began his tenure in AD 26, was removed for the same reason in AD 36, on account of his massacre of Samaritans. The Jewish philosopher Philo writes that Pontius Pilate was a man of "vindictiveness and furious temper." From the start, Pilate took a stand of antagonism and disdain for the Jews. In blatant disregard for the Jewish prohibition on graven images and the usual Roman tolerance for their religious sensitivities, he ordered standard banners bearing the image of the 'divine' emperor to be placed in Jerusalem. This had to be done at night because of the public outcry that could ensue; and, sure enough, the inhabitants of Jerusalem rose up the next morning in great numbers to protest. They remained there for five days, and he surrounded them with his soldiers ready to perpetrate a massacre. At last he relented, but he would have plenty of other occasions to shed the blood of rebellious Jews throughout his 10 years in office.

The hearing before the Sanhedrin had focused on religious matters. Now the members of the Sanhedrin, likely with the exception of Joseph of Arimathea and Nicodemus, pushed for the death penalty on grounds that such a sentence would appeal to Pilate as a Roman authority who was unconcerned with points of Jewish religion. In this venue, Jesus would have few rights since he was a provincial and not a Roman citizen. Thus, the Romans could do as they pleased with him. The religious authorities charged, "We found this man misleading our people; he opposes the payment of taxes to Caesar and maintains that he is the Messiah, a king" (Lk. 23:2). Pilate asked Jesus, "Are you the king of the Jews?" If he were indeed making himself king, this would be apart from Roman rule and represent one of the sporadic revolutionary movements among the Jews. Jesus answered, "You say so." According to Hahn and Mitch, Jesus answered in this way since, while he was a king in a heavenly sense, he was not the type of king they had in mind.

We read, "Pilate then addressed the chief priests and the crowds, 'I find this man not guilty.'" Jesus, in fact, had not opposed paying taxes to Rome. But Pilate already knew something was up; he knew that the Jews were not ones to hand over one of their own to the Romans for opposing taxes to Caesar, or even for being a king. Therefore, it is not surprising that Pilate knew Jesus was innocent of these charges and that this was about something else, even though procuring justice was probably not a particular interest of his. The Jews would typically be sympathetic to such movements. The members of the Sanhedrin, of course, were not happy with his initial judgment, but their remonstration unwittingly gave Pilate a way out. They retorted, "He is inciting the people with his teaching throughout all Judea, from Galilee where he began even to here."

"Galilee" – this gave Pilate an idea. Herod Antipas, who ruled Galilee and Perea from his capital of Tiberias on the western shore of the Sea of Galilee, was in Jerusalem for the feast of the Passover; he was a Jew by religion, though an Edomite by birth. If Jesus was from Galilee and had committed many of the alleged infractions there, then surely he should be tried by Herod. Furthermore, Herod, even though he had killed the prophet John the Baptist, would know more about the Jewish religion, even if he didn't have much regard for living its laws. But most importantly for Pilate, whatever decision Herod made would be attributed to the latter in the event that either Jesus' supporters or his enemies should riot as a result.

Only the Gospel of Luke mentions Jesus being sent to Herod, and later a prayer of the Jerusalem Christian community in the Book of Acts alludes to it (Acts 4:27). All the Synoptic Gospels speak of Herod's intrigue with Jesus because of his miracles. When Jesus was brought before him, Luke tells us that he was glad because he hoped Jesus would put on a supernatural spectacle for him. Instead, Jesus said nothing, submitting to his sacrificial destiny and refusing even to answer the charges brought against him. Not getting his miracle, Herod began to deride Jesus. We read, "Herod and his soldiers treated him contemptuously and mocked him, and after clothing him in resplendent garb, he sent him back to Pilate"

(Lk. 23:11). Certainly he did not believe the charge that Jesus was establishing a kingship opposed to the established authorities; thus, he mocked both Jesus and the allegation.

Pilate was dismayed to see that Jesus was returned to him, though Luke tells us that the day's interaction forged an alliance between Pilate and Herod. The Gospels portray Pilate as reluctant to crucify Jesus and insistent on Jesus' innocence of the charges brought against him. As N. T. Wright suggests, Pilate's actual motive for this response may not have been the justice of Jesus' cause but his own contempt for the Jewish authorities and unwillingness to accept readily whatever they might propose. Jesus might potentially get in the way of the Romans, but scourging him would certainly deter him from making any further trouble and might appease the crowd. The Gospel of John places the scourging of Jesus before the sentence of death because Pilate might have hoped by this measure to appease the crowd's sentiments against Jesus so that crucifying him would not be necessary. The Synoptic Gospels, however, place it after the sentence of death; the Romans typically first scourged those condemned to crucifixion. Roman scourging was a particularly terrible thing because the whip – the *flagellum* – had multiple leather strands lined with many sharp objects that would cut into the victim's bare flesh. The Church historian Eusebius of Caesarea (d. 339) tells us, of the Roman scourging of later Christian martyrs, that "the bystanders were struck with amazement when they saw them lacerated with scourges even to the innermost veins and arteries, so that the hidden inward parts of the body, both their bowels and their members, were exposed to view" (*Church History* 4.15.4). Roman citizens were exempt from the penalties of scourging and crucifixion, which were reserved for slaves and provincials.

Matthew's Gospel tells us that Pilate would release one prisoner the Jews wanted each year during the feast of Passover. All the Gospels tell us that the choice was between Jesus and Barabbas; they contrast the innocence of Jesus with the lawlessness of Barabbas, representing the lawlessness of humanity. John says Barabbas was a revolutionary, and Luke tells us he was "imprisoned for rebellion and murder" (Lk. 23:25). It is possible that, rather than being a common criminal, Barabbas was a kind of terrorist fighting Roman rule by any means. The religious authorities incited the crowd to release Barabbas and to crucify Jesus. Crucifixion in all its horror was designed to be the penalty for terrorist rebels such as Barabbas, not for wandering philosophers or prophets like Jesus. Yet the Gospels show how Jesus symbolically traded places with Barabbas. Meanwhile, Jesus' supporters and followers were scattered, afraid of what might be done to them if they showed support for Jesus.

Pilate, at least in the earthly sense, was in full control of whether or not Jesus was crucified, but ultimately he was more concerned with politics than with justice. He granted the crowd's demand for Jesus to be crucified while at the same time admitting Jesus' innocence of the charges. Famously, he washed his hands of Jesus' blood. Such a gesture was common among the Romans for insisting upon innocence of an evil deed. N. T. Wright proposes, though, that Pilate was really performing the deed in jest or for show –

that he was really just trying to make an appearance of disdain for the wishes of the Jewish authorities.

The Roman soldiers who took Jesus were likewise not concerned with Jesus' innocence in their treatment of him. They were accustomed of making sport of condemned prisoners. We read, "The soldiers led him away inside the palace, that is, the praetorium, and assembled the whole cohort. They clothed him in purple and, weaving a crown of thorns, placed it on him. They began to salute him with, 'Hail, King of the Jews!' and kept striking his head with a reed and spitting upon him. They knelt before him in homage. And when they had mocked him, they stripped him of the purple cloak, dressed him in his own clothes, and led him out to crucify him" (Mk. 15:16-20). A cohort consisted of 600 soldiers, so the mocking of Jesus was no small spectacle. It was the entertainment for the day. Their ultimate interest was not so much in Jesus personally as in the Jews in general. Here they had one of them in their power without knowing who he really was. They gloried in the apparent victory of Rome over this pitiful 'King of the Jews.'

The Crucifixion of Jesus

Crucifixion was one of the worst forms of punishment, intended to induce not only long hours of torture before death but also total humiliation. Used by previous empires as an extreme deterrent, the Romans commonly executed slaves, revolutionaries, and heinous criminals in this way. Jesus' manifest innocence in no way mitigated the barbarous behavior of the soldiers, who were accustomed to getting the job done in the cruelest way possible.

After the scourging, the execution began with the victim carrying a hundred-pound wooden crossbeam on his shoulders, often falling to the ground because of his already-weakened state. The soldiers forced a passer-by named Simon of Cyrene to help Jesus carry his cross; soldiers would often force civilians to perform tasks for them. Interestingly, Mark mentions that Simon was "the father of Alexander and Rufus," which may imply that he and his sons later became believers known among the early Christian community (Mk. 15:21).

Jesus' trial had begun around 6 o'clock in the morning, his carrying of the cross around 8 o'clock, and then his crucifixion around 9 o'clock in the morning. Jerusalem would have been at its busiest because of all the pilgrims who had come for the feast of Passover. Since Jesus hung on the cross from 9 o'clock in the morning to 3 o'clock in the afternoon, a great many people would have witnessed it. While many jeered at Jesus during his passion, many were also sympathetic towards him. Luke tells us, "A large crowd of people followed Jesus, including many women who mourned and lamented him" (Lk. 23:27). Despite his agony, Jesus continued to prophesy, saying to the women, "Daughters of Jerusalem, do not weep for me; weep instead for yourselves and for your children, for indeed, the days are coming when people will say, 'Blessed are the barren, the wombs that never bore and the breasts that never nursed.' At that time people will say to the mountains, 'Fall upon us!' and to the hills, 'Cover us!' for if these things are done when the wood is green what will happen when it is dry?" (Lk. 23:28-31). He spoke honorably of the women in calling them by the biblical title of favor 'daughters of Jerusalem.' The olive tree was a symbol of Jerusalem, thus the mention of 'wood.' According to Hahn and Mitch, "As long as the city is like green wood, which is moist and unsuitable for making a fire, there is still time to repent and embrace the Messiah. Persistent rebellion, however, will make Jerusalem dry and fit to be burned." The city was indeed destroyed in AD 70 by the Romans, following rebellion. The Christians fled and were spared because of Jesus' prophecies about what was to take place due to God's judgment.

The destination for Jesus was Golgatha, meaning the 'Place of the Skull,' which, translated through Latin to English, is often called 'Calvary.' Major cities in the Roman Empire typically had sites for crucifixion outside the walls, where the vertical stakes of the crosses were permanently positioned. This is likely the kind of site that Golgotha had become in the time of Jesus. Prior to nailing victims to the cross, soldiers would often offer them drugged wine to deaden some of the pain. Jesus, however, refused this wine, perhaps because he desired to experience the full pain since he bore the weight of the punishment for the sins of the world.

Various theories exist about the specifics of Roman crucifixion, based on the many ancient accounts documenting it. When the victims arrived at the site, they would be stripped and nailed to the crossbeam, likely through the wrists, and then hoisted onto the vertical stake before having each heel nailed to the side of the stake. Soldiers most likely retrieved the five- to- seven-inch iron nails from the bodies to reuse. However, one first-century crucified heel bone was discovered by archaeologists in Jerusalem in 1968 with the tip of the nail bent backward as it was driven into the wood; thus, the victim, named Jehohanan, was buried with the nail still attached to the heel. His bones were then preserved in an ossuary since his family had apparently had his remains spared from the usual lot of being cast into a mass grave. There were traces of olive wood on the nail from the cross, and it was clear that the feet had been nailed separately to the side of the crossbeam. Nonetheless, the Romans would often crucify victims in different positions and invent various ways of mocking them.

Part of the particular sport to which Jesus was subject was wearing the crown of thorns, which he had received during the ordeal before the cohort. Victims typically were given inscriptions that announced their crime so as to deter others from committing similar offenses. They may have had to wear these inscriptions around their necks while carrying their crosses, before having them fixed over their heads while on the cross itself. Jesus' inscription, written in Latin, Greek, and Aramaic so that all passers-by would understand, is translated, "Jesus of Nazareth, King of the Jews." One might also wonder if he was placed in the center between the two robbers in connection with the charge of being a king, stripped and suspended in air on the cross rather than seated in splendid garments on a royal throne.

The Sacrificial Death of Jesus

Suspended on the cross, breathing itself was a torture because each breath required pressure placed on the nailed hands and feet. Thus Jesus' words on the cross were few, but they were deep and deliberate. We read in Mark, "And at around three o'clock Jesus cried out in a loud voice, *'Eloi, Eloi, lema sabachthani?'* which is translated, 'My God, my God, why have you forsaken me?'" (Mk. 15:34). These are the first lines of Psalm 22, a psalm that seems to point to Jesus' suffering on the cross. There we read, "All who see me mock me; they curl their lips and jeer; they shake their heads at me: 'You relied on the Lord – let him deliver you; if he loves you, let him rescue you" (Ps. 22:8-9). In a similar fashion, Jesus was mocked on the cross by passers-by, by the chief priests, by the soldiers, and even by the criminals crucified with him. Only his disciple John, his mother Mary, and several women followers bravely stood there with him in his support. The psalm continues, "Yea, dogs are round about me; a company of evildoers encircle me; they have pierced my hands and feet – I can count all my bones – they stare and gloat over me; they divide my garments among them, and for my raiment they cast lots" (Ps. 22:16-18 [RSV]). Accordingly, the soldiers cast lots for Jesus' tunic rather than tear it in parts since it was a single fabric (Jn. 19:23-24). The psalm concludes with the end result of the suffering: "All the ends of the earth will worship and turn to the LORD... I will live for the LORD; my descendants will serve you. The generation to come will be told of the LORD, that they may proclaim to a people yet unborn the deliverance you have brought" (Ps. 22:28, 31-32). Thus, Jesus' prayer, while being one of distress, was not at all one of despair.

Mark tells us that the criminals crucified with Jesus were revolutionaries, and Matthew tells us that they both reviled Jesus. The word Mark uses actually means 'robbers,' but Josephus uses that word to refer to ideological brigands who would sabotage imperial interests in the interests of Jewish freedom. Such men would have had little use for Jesus, who preached a kingdom of peace. One of the criminals had a change of heart since Luke quotes him as saying, "Have you no fear of God...? ... And indeed, we have been condemned justly, for the sentence we received corresponds to our crimes, but this man has done nothing criminal. ... Jesus, remember me when you come into your kingdom" (Lk. 23:40-42). Jesus said to him, "Amen, I say to you, today you will be with me in Paradise" (Lk. 23:43).

While Jesus did not accept the wine drugged with myrrh just before being nailed to the cross, the Gospel of John tells us that Jesus said from the cross, around three o'clock, "I thirst." Mother Teresa placed these words at the center of her spirituality, understanding them to indicate Jesus' thirst for souls. John tells us, "There was a vessel filled with common wine. So they put a sponge soaked in wine on a sprig of hyssop and put it up to his mouth" (Jn. 19:29). Hyssop, again, alludes to sacrifice, and this was the moment of sacrifice for the paschal lambs in the Temple. Brant Pitre, in his book *Jesus and the Jewish Roots of the Eucharist*, states his belief that this wine was the fourth cup of the Passover Seder that Jesus had not drunk at the time, thus showing the seamless connection of the Last Supper and Jesus' death on the cross. Jesus had said at his Last Supper that "from this time on I shall not drink of the fruit of the vine until the kingdom of God comes" (Lk. 22:18), and he had prayed in the Garden of Gethsemane for the Father to "take this cup away from me; still not my will but yours be done" (Lk. 22:42). But after he drank this sour wine, he said, "It is finished" (Jn. 19:30). The Gospel of Luke tells us, "Jesus cried out in a loud vice, 'Father, into your hands I commend my spirit'" (Lk. 23:46). And then he died.

Victims of crucifixion often lingered on for hours or even days as they wasted away and endured the elements. Death could come in a number of ways, including asphyxiation because of the extreme difficulty in breathing while suspended on the cross. Typically the Romans would leave the bodies on the cross after death to decay, thus adding to the horror of crucifixion even after death. Jesus, however, was crucified on the day of preparation before the first day of Passover – the day on which the Seder meal was to be celebrated and for which Jews had to purify themselves. Bodies hanging on the cross would bring defilement to the Passover, which also coincided that year with the Sabbath. So the soldiers smashed the legs of the two robbers with an iron club to rapidly hasten asphyxiation; they could not breathe in that position without the use of their legs. Jesus, however, had already died. John tells us that a soldier thrust a lance into his side to confirm his death, and blood and water gushed forth, symbolizing the blessings won by Christ's death. Pope Benedict interprets the blood and water as further symbolizing the sacraments of Eucharist and Baptism.

Pope Benedict writes of the dramatic events after Jesus' death, "The Synoptic Gospels explicitly portray Jesus' death on the Cross as a cosmic event: the sun is darkened, the veil of the Temple is torn in two, the earth quakes, and the dead rise." Mark tells us the veil of the Temple was torn from top to bottom at Jesus' death. There were two veils in the Temple to block outsiders from entering the holiest of chambers. One separated the Holy of Holies from the rest of the sanctuary, and the other separated the sanctuary from the outer courts. According to Hahn and Mitch, "Although the evangelist does not specify which of the two veils was torn, the lesson to be learned is clear: access to the Father is now open through Jesus, who as high priest has entered on our behalf." Meanwhile the Gospel of Mark, in which the narrative leads up to the question of Jesus' true identity, climaxes with the confession of the centurion responsible for carrying out the execution: "Truly this man was the Son of God!" (Mk. 15:39).

The Burial of Jesus

The lot for condemned criminals was burial in a common grave. However, Joseph of Arimathea, a member of the Sanhedrin but a secret supporter of Jesus, realized that the tomb he had purchased for himself was in a garden close to the place where Jesus was crucified and would be ideal for the burial. So Joseph found courage enough to go to Pilate and ask for Jesus' body. Pilate gave him permission to take it, and we are told that Joseph had Jesus buried in his own new tomb. In fact, it was close enough to the site of Jesus' crucifixion that the Church of the Holy Sepulcher in Jerusalem is able to house the traditional sites of both Jesus' crucifixion and his tomb. Joseph's offer was exceptionally generous. He wanted to give Jesus a burial worthy of a prophet and provide a site where his followers could pray in his memory in future years, as was common at the graves of the prophets. We are told that a large stone was rolled across the entrance. This indicates that it was not a common tomb but actually quite rare; only the wealthy could afford such burial places, which were only made for a short period of history. Since Joseph was a member of the Sanhedrin, it is further likely that, as William Lane Craig suggests in his book *The*

Son Rises, the tombs of some important Jewish leaders were nearby in the garden.

The corpse was not to remain forever laid out in the tomb. Instead, after a period of time, the bones would be gathered and placed in an ossuary to allow room for more bodies to be buried. Thus, people were not always buried in new tombs. From a Jewish perspective, it could only be that way in Jesus' case since a condemned criminal could not be buried with other bodies without defiling them. But it was actually providential and a sign of Christ's holiness; we might recall that Jesus was conceived in a virginal womb and that he rode into Jerusalem on a donkey no one had ever ridden before.

Since Jesus was buried on the day of preparation, time was of the essence, for with sundown came the Sabbath (which further coincided with Passover in John's account), during which no work could be done. There was barely time enough to buy a linen shroud, wash and wrap the body, and bury it in the tomb. Since Joseph of Arimathea was a wealthy man, Craig says it is likely that his servants carried out the tasks surrounding the burial, given especially that there were only a few hours between Jesus' death and sundown. Furthermore, anyone planning on celebrating the Passover the next day would be rendered ritually unclean for the celebration by entering the tomb or handling the body. The Gospel of John tells us that Nicodemus, another wealthy supporter of Jesus from among the religious authorities, came with 100 pounds of myrrh and aloes for Jesus' burial, likewise probably transported by his servants. This was another highly generous gift, far beyond the ordinary. Given that the Romans, at the demands of the Sanhedrin, had degraded Jesus' body, these wealthy supporters of Jesus from the Sanhedrin did what they could to see to it that he at least had a burial fit for a king. What they could not do was bring Jesus back.

Most of Jesus' apostles, however, stayed well out of the public eye, not even attempting to attend the burial or visit the tomb. Since there was some talk about Jesus' prophesy that he would rise after three days, Matthew tells us, the religious authorities asked Pilate to place a guard of soldiers in front of the tomb for security. These sentries would see to it that nothing would happen and that no one could steal the body to feign a miraculous event. To the apostles' minds, therefore, going to the tomb amounted to walking into a trap. Stealing the body was the last of their concerns. Number one was simply staying alive by lying low – unlike Jesus, who had spoken out boldly and now was dead. They no longer knew quite what to make of Jesus. How could he have offered such powerful teachings and awe-inspiring miracles only to be captured and promptly executed in the most shameful way possible? What would they do now with their lives? Perhaps they didn't even get that far in their thinking, so consumed were they by grief for this man to whom they had become so attached, by regret for their failure to protect or support him, and by fear of what might lie ahead for them. The disciples on the road to Emmaus later echoed their sentiments: "But we were hoping that he would be the one to redeem Israel" (Lk. 24:21).

The Resurrection and Beyond

Jesus had once prophesied, "Just as Jonah was in the belly of the whale three days and three nights, so will the Son of Man be in the heart of the earth three days and three nights" (Mt. 12:40). In the Old Testament, the third day was often when God acted with power. If the religious authorities feared that something might come of Jesus' prophesy about rising in three days, the disciples were too numb and frightened for much anticipation of their own. Mary Magdalen likely felt the same way as she approached the tomb on the morning of the first day of the week (Sunday morning) to anoint the body with spices. She and the other women remained true to Jesus through his sufferings, comforting him and then mourning him after his death. Now they wished to do whatever might be possible to normalize this dreadful situation, as the flashbacks of his unjust execution haunted their imaginations. Mark tells us that a number of women had stayed and witnessed the crucifixion. Some of these also went to the tomb, and each of the Gospels mentions Mary Magdalen as being at the tomb. The Gospels directly tell us that Jesus had driven out seven demons from her. Medieval tradition identified Mary Magdalen as the sinful woman who anointed the feet of Jesus (Mk. 14:3-9), but many scholars doubt this identification, which is not made in the Gospels. Given her name, it is possible that she was from Magdala on the western shore of the Sea of Galilee. Mary, the mother of James (the apostle), is also mentioned as being at the tomb by Mark, Luke, and possibly Matthew, who speaks of "the other Mary." Luke mentions Joanna, and Mark mentions Salome. Richard Bauckham, in *Jesus and the Eyewitnesses*, says that while they were all likely present, the ones through whom the various Gospel writers received their oral accounts were likely the ones recorded in those particular Gospels.

These women were faithful disciples of Jesus, some of whom had experienced his miraculous healing in their own lives. We read in Luke's Gospel that, during Jesus' ministry in Galilee, "Accompanying him were the Twelve and some women who had been cured of evil spirits and infirmities, Mary, called Magdalene, from whom seven demons had gone out, Joanna, the wife of Herod's steward Chuza, Susanna, and many others who provided for them out of their resources"

(Lk. 8:1-3). Some of these were about to experience the miracle of all miracles.

The women went to the tomb early in the morning. Given that they had missed critical time due to the Passover, they wanted to make sure that the body would be anointed before much decay. They would also avoid the crowds that were still in Jerusalem for the Passover and abuzz with opinions about Jesus and what had happened to him. Luke tells us, "But at daybreak on the first day of the week they took the spices they had prepared and went to the tomb. They found the stone rolled away from the tomb; but when they entered, they did not find the body of the Lord Jesus. While they were puzzling over this, behold, two men in dazzling garments appeared to them. They were terrified and bowed their faces to the ground. They said to them, 'Why do you seek the living one among the dead? He is not here, but he has been raised'" (Lk. 24:1-5).

Any first-century Jew making up a fabulous story would certainly not have listed women as the first witnesses of the supposed event. The Gospel writers handed it on that way because that is what actually happened. Craig writes, "The fact that women, whose witness counted for nothing, are said to have discovered the empty tomb makes it very credible historically that such was the case. ... it is equally unlikely that the early believers would have made up the story of the disciples' hiding in cowardice, while women boldly observed the crucifixion and burial and visited the tomb. The early believers would have no motive in humiliating its leaders by making them into cowards and women into heroes." We may find further meaning in the providential fact that women first witnessed the Resurrection: it shows the high esteem that Jesus gave to women; it rewarded the women for their faithfulness at Calvary; and it was a connection to the healing and newness of life that Jesus had already brought about in their own lives. Thus, St. Augustine called Mary Magdalen the 'apostle to the Apostles.'

While the disciples at first did not know what to make of the women's story, Peter and the 'other disciple whom Jesus loved,' namely John, ran to the tomb to investigate. In the Gospel of John we read, "They both ran, but the other disciple ran faster than Peter and arrived at the tomb first; he bent down and saw the burial cloths there, but did not go in"John, who was likely younger than Peter, saw that something great and powerful had happened, so he deferred to Peter, who was not only his elder but also the leader of the apostles. We read, "When Simon Peter arrived after him, he went into the tomb and saw the burial cloths there, and the cloth that had covered his head, not with the burial cloths but rolled up in a separate place" (Jn. 20:6-7). Tomb raiders were common in the day. What was of value was not the body itself but the expensive burial cloths, however, so the disappearance of Jesus' body was not due to theft.

Still, no one had actually seen Jesus as yet. Soon enough, Jesus would appear to Mary Magdalen, to two disciples on the road from Jerusalem to Emmaus, and then to the apostles. In fact, St. Paul wrote that Jesus appeared "to more than five hundred people, most of whom are still living" (1 Cor. 15:6). Just as the Gospel writers listed the witnesses by name so that readers could consult them, Paul likely wrote about the witnesses "who are still living" so that they could be asked about their experience of Jesus. Craig points out that if Jesus had not truly been raised, the disciples would never have been able to proclaim the resurrection of Jesus in Jerusalem, where Jesus' enemies would certainly be able to go to the tomb, take out the body, and parade it about to crush the rumors. Instead, the religious authorities admitted the empty tomb but accused the disciples of stealing the body to feign resurrection. Matthew tells us that they bribed the soldiers guarding the tomb to spread their version of the story: "You are to say, 'His disciples came by night and stole him while we were asleep.' And if this gets to the ears of the governor, we will satisfy [him] and keep you out of trouble" (Mt. 28:13-14).

After his resurrection, Jesus was changed in appearance so that his friends did not at first recognize him. He could walk through the doors that his disciples had locked to keep out the religious authorities. At the same time, he could eat, drink, and breathe, and he emphasized that his body was a true body; he was not a ghost. Yet he retained the marks of his wounds as if they were badges of honor, which they were. The resurrection of Jesus was something entirely new, unlike even Jesus' miracles of raising Lazarus, the son of the widow of Nain, and Jarius' daughter. As Pope Benedict says, it was in some ways like "an evolutionary leap" for the human race. He had new power to give. Thus, we read in John, "he breathed on [his apostles] and said to them, 'Receive the holy Spirit. Whose sins you forgive are forgiven them, and whose sins you retain are retained'" (Jn. 20:22-23).

Jesus walked among his disciples for 40 days before ascending to Heaven. He told his disciples to wait in Jerusalem for the coming of the Holy Spirit. We read in the Acts of the Apostles, "When they had gathered together they asked him, 'Lord, are you at this time going to restore the kingdom to Israel?' He answered them, 'It is not for you to know the times or seasons that the Father has established by his own authority. But you will receive power when the Holy Spirit comes upon you, and you will be my witnesses in Jerusalem, throughout Judea and Samaria, and to the ends of the earth.' When he had said this, as they were looking on, he was lifted up, and a cloud took him from their sight" (Acts 1:6-9).

The disciples weren't the only ones waiting for something. During the 49 days between Passover and Pentecost, the Jews would 'count the omer' each day, marking their anticipation of the coming of God's Law by way of the ancient measure of barley. Pentecost looks back to God's revelation of the Law to Israel at Mt. Sinai. However, the disciples didn't quite know what to expect in their own anticipation. We read in the Book of Acts, "When the time for Pentecost was fulfilled, they were all in one place together. And suddenly there came from the sky a noise like a strong driving wind, and it filled the entire house in which they were. There appeared to them tongues as of fire, which parted and came to rest on each one of them" (Acts 2:1-3). We might think of the scene at Mt. Sinai before God delivered the Law: "Mount Sinai was all wrapped in smoke, for the LORD came down upon it in fire" (Ex. 19:18). For St. Thomas Aquinas, the indwelling of the Holy Spirit in the soul is itself the New Law. The Holy Spirit, sent by Jesus and the Father, was the One who Jesus said "will teach you everything and remind you of all that [I] have told you" (Jn. 14:26). The Holy Spirit is that same Spirit of God who, we are told, "was moving over the face of the waters" at creation (Gen. 1:2 [RSV]).

The apostles, who up to this point were highly doubtful and fearful, were suddenly changed. They were now certain of their faith and ready to proclaim it boldly. Peter and the others immediately went out and preached. Pentecost was a pilgrimage feast, so Jews from all over were in Jerusalem, but they each heard the apostles in their own language even though the latter were speaking Aramaic with a Galilean accent. We read, "Peter [said] to them, 'Repent and be baptized, every one of you, in the name of Jesus Christ for the forgiveness of your sins; and you will receive the gift of the holy Spirit.' ... Those who accepted his message were baptized, and about three thousand persons were added that day" (Acts 2:38, 41).

After that, we read, "They devoted themselves to the teaching of the apostles and to the communal life, to the breaking of the bread and to the prayers. Awe came upon everyone, and many wonders and signs were done through the apostles" (Acts 2:42-43). Even after Jesus rose again, the disciples did not fully understand what God's plan really was. But with the gift of the Holy Spirit at Pentecost, they understood that God's will was the growth and formation of God's New Covenant people, awaiting Christ's Second Coming.

Epilogue

Just as Jesus was a polarizing figure in his day, requiring a response of either faith or doubt, so he challenges us today with that same choice. The leap of faith is not a blind leap but more like a trust-fall, done in knowledge that your companions will only ask you to fall if they know they will catch you. Faith is a response to God, who has shown himself to be reasonable. The Christian faith is not one that is based on far-fetched legends but on an event – the 'Christ-event' – that happened in history and that can be as thoroughly supported by the evidence as anything that happened 2,000 years ago can be. But after showing himself to be reasonable, God does require a response of faith. As Craig reminds us, while much evidence could be given for the resurrection, simple historical acceptance would miss the point. As Jesus said to the apostle Thomas, who at first doubted the resurrection, "Have you come to believe because you have seen me? Blessed are those who have not seen and have believed" (Jn. 20:29). Some disciples even doubted after seeing the resurrected Jesus with their own eyes. We read at the end of the Gospel of Matthew, "When they saw him, they worshiped, but they doubted" (Mt. 28:17). They needed further help from God's grace, which they would receive at Pentecost.

Faith involves a relationship of trust in God who reveals. Thus, history only goes so far; to experience the rest, you must jump!

Appendix: Herod's Temple

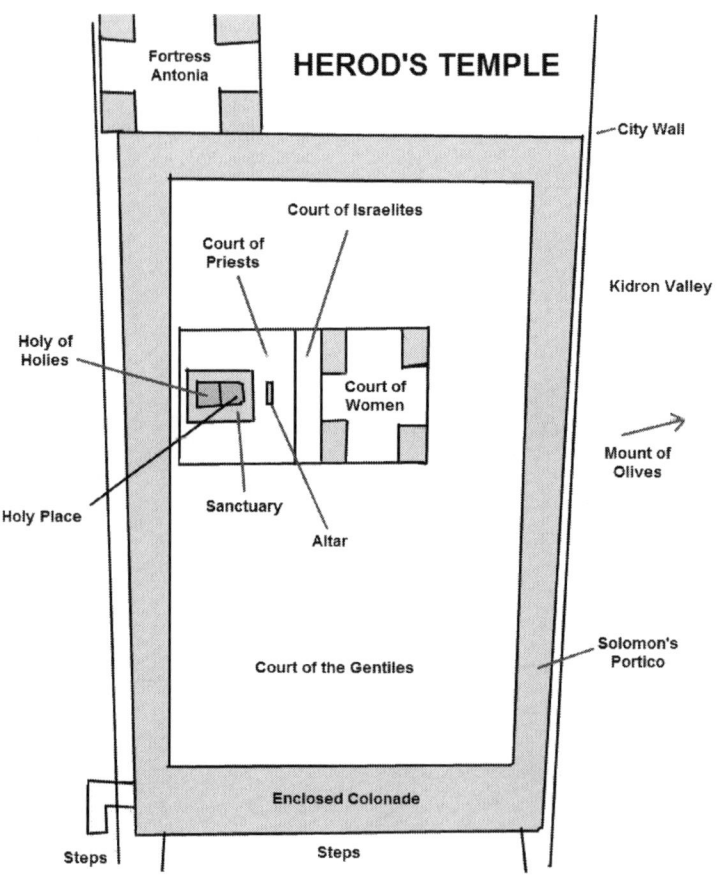

Please enjoy the first two chapters of Pope Francis: Pastor of Mercy, also written by Michael J. Ruszala, as available from Wyatt North Publishing.

Pope Francis: Pastor of Mercy

Chapter 1

There is something about Pope Francis that captivates and delights people, even people who hardly know anything about him. He was elected in only two days of the conclave, yet many who tried their hand at speculating on who the next pope might be barely included him on their lists. The evening of Wednesday, March 13, 2013, the traditional white smoke poured out from the chimney of the Sistine Chapel and spread throughout the world by way of television, Internet, radio, and social media, signaling the beginning of a new papacy.

As the light of day waned from the Eternal City, some 150,000 people gathered watching intently for any movement behind the curtained door to the loggia of St. Peter's. A little after 8:00 p.m., the doors swung open and Cardinal Tauran emerged to pronounce the traditional and joyous Latin formula to introduce the new Bishop of Rome: "Annuncio vobis gaudium magnum; habemus papam!" ("I announce to you a great joy: we have a pope!") He then announced the new Holy Father's identity: "Cardinalem Bergoglio..."

The name Bergoglio, stirred up confusion among most of the faithful who flooded the square that were even more clueless than the television announcers were, who scrambled to figure out who exactly the new pope was. Pausing briefly, Cardinal Tauran continued by announcing the name of the new pope: "...qui sibi nomen imposuit Franciscum" ("who takes for himself the name Francis"). Whoever this man may be, his name choice resonated with all, and the crowd erupted with jubilant cheers. A few moments passed before the television announcers and their support teams informed their global audiences that the man who was about to walk onto the loggia dressed in white was Cardinal Jorge Mario Bergoglio, age 76, of Buenos Aires, Argentina.

To add to the bewilderment and kindling curiosity, when the new pope stepped out to the thunderous applause of the crowd in St. Peter's Square, he did not give the expected papal gesture of outstretched arms. Instead, he gave only a simple and modest wave. Also, before giving his first apostolic blessing, he bowed asking the faithful, from the least to the greatest, to silently pray for him. These acts were only the beginning of many more words and gestures, such as taking a seat on the bus with the cardinals, refusing a popemobile with bulletproof glass, and paying his own hotel bill after his election, that would raise eyebrows among some familiar with papal customs and delight the masses.

Is he making a pointed critique of previous pontificates? Is he simply posturing a persona to the world at large to make a point? The study of the life of Jorge Mario Bergoglio gives a clear answer, and the answer is no. This is simply who he is as a man and as a priest. The example of his thought-provoking gestures flows from his character, his life experiences, his religious vocation, and his spirituality. This book uncovers the life of the 266th Bishop of Rome, Jorge Mario Bergoglio, also known as Father Jorge, a name he preferred even while he was an archbishop and cardinal.

What exactly do people find so attractive about Pope Francis? Aldo Cagnoli, a layman who developed a friendship with the Pope when he was serving as a cardinal, shares the following: "The greatness of the man, in my humble opinion lies not in building walls or seeking refuge behind his wisdom and office, but rather in dealing with everyone judiciously, respectfully, and with humility, being willing to learn at any moment of life; that is what Father Bergoglio means to me" (as quoted in Ch. 12 of Pope Francis:

Conversations with Jorge Bergoglio, previously published as *El Jesuita* [*The Jesuit*]).

At World Youth Day 2013, in Rio de Janeiro, Brazil, three million young people came out to celebrate their faith with Pope Francis. Doug Barry, from EWTN's Life on the Rock, interviewed youth at the event on what features stood out to them about Pope Francis. The young people seemed most touched by his authenticity. One young woman from St. Louis said, "He really knows his audience. He doesn't just say things to say things... And he is really sincere and genuine in all that he does." A friend agreed: "He was looking out into the crowd and it felt like he was looking at each one of us...." A young man from Canada weighed in: "You can actually relate to [him]... for example, last night he was talking about the World Cup and athletes." A young woman added, "I feel he means what he says... he practices what he preaches... he states that he's there for the poor and he actually means it."

The Holy Spirit guided the College of Cardinals in its election of Pope Francis to meet the needs of the Church following the historic resignation of Pope Benedict XVI due to old age. Representing the growth and demographic shift in the Church throughout the world and especially in the Southern

Hemisphere, Pope Francis is the first non-European pope in almost 1,300 years. He is also the first Jesuit pope. Pope Francis comes with a different background and set of experiences. Both as archbishop and as pope, his flock knows him for his humility, ascetic frugality in solidarity with the poor, and closeness. He was born in Buenos Aires to a family of Italian immigrants, earned a diploma in chemistry, and followed a priestly vocation in the Jesuit order after an experience of God's mercy while receiving the sacrament of Reconciliation. Even though he is known for his smile and humor, the world also recognizes Pope Francis as a stern figure that stands against the evils of the world and challenges powerful government officials, when necessary.

The Church he leads is one that has been burdened in the West by the aftermath of sex abuse scandals and increased secularism. It is also a Church that is experiencing shifting in numbers out of the West and is being challenged with religious persecution in the Middle East, Asia, and Africa. The Vatican that Pope Francis has inherited is plagued by cronyism and scandal. This Holy Father knows, however, that his job is not merely about numbers, politics, or even success. He steers clear of pessimism knowing that he is the head of Christ's Body on earth and works with Christ's grace. This is the man God has chosen in these times to lead his flock.

Chapter 2: Early Life in Argentina

Jorge Mario Bergoglio was born on December 17, 1936, in the Flores district of Buenos Aires. The district was a countryside locale outside the main city during the nineteenth century and many rich people in its early days called this place home. By the time Jorge was born, Flores was incorporated into the city of Buenos Aires and became a middle class neighborhood. Flores is also the home of the beautiful Romantic-styled Basilica of San José de Flores, built in 1831, with its dome over the altar, spire over the entrance, and columns at its facade. It was the Bergoglios' parish church and had much significance in Jorge's life.

Jorge's father's family had arrived in Argentina in 1929, immigrating from Piedimonte in northern Italy. They were not the only ones immigrating to the country. In the late nineteenth century, Argentina became industrialized and the government promoted immigration from Europe. During that time, the land prospered and Buenos Aires earned the moniker "Paris of the South." In the late nineteenth and early twentieth centuries waves of immigrants from Italy, Spain, and other European countries came off ships in the port of Buenos Aires. Three of Jorge's great uncles were the first in the family to immigrate to Argentina in 1922 searching for better employment opportunities after World War I. They established a paving company in Buenos Aires and built a four-story building for their company with the city's first elevator. Jorge's father and paternal grandparents followed the brothers in order to keep the family together and to escape Mussolini's fascist regime in Italy. Jorge's father and grandfather also helped with the business for a time. His father, Mario, who had been an accountant for a rail company in Italy, provided similar services for the family business (Cardinal Bergoglio recalls more on the story of his family's immigration and his early life in Ch. 1 of Conversations with Jorge Bergoglio).

Providentially, the Bergoglios were long delayed in liquidating their assets in Italy; this forced them to miss the ship they planned to sail on, the doomed Pricipessa Mafalda, which sank off the northern coast of Brazil before reaching Buenos Aires. The family took the Giulio Cesare instead and arrived safely in Argentina with Jorge's Grandma Rosa. Grandma Rosa wore a fur coat stuffed with the money the family brought with them from Italy. Economic hard times eventually hit Argentina in 1932 and the family's paving business went under, but the Bergoglio brothers began anew.

Jorge's father, Mario, met his mother Regina at Mass in 1934. Regina was born in Argentina, but her parents were also Italian immigrants. Mario and Regina married the following year after meeting. Jorge, the eldest of their five children, was born in 1936. Jorge fondly recalls his mother gathering the children around the radio on Sunday afternoons to listen to opera and explain the story. A true porteño, as the inhabitants of the port city of Buenos Aires are called, Jorge liked to play soccer, listen to Latin music, and dance the tango. Jorge's paternal grandparents lived around the corner from his home. He greatly admired his Grandma Rosa, and keeps her written prayer for her grandchildren with him until this day. Jorge recalls that while his grandparents kept their personal conversations in Piedmontese, Mario chose mostly to speak Spanish, preferring to look forward rather than back. Still, Jorge grew up speaking both Italian and Spanish.

Upon entering secondary school at the age of thirteen, his father insisted that Jorge begin work even though the family, in their modest lifestyle, was not particularly in need of extra income. Mario Bergoglio wanted to teach the boy the value of work and found several jobs for him during his adolescent years. Jorge worked in a hosiery factory for several years as a cleaner and at a desk. When he entered technical school to study food chemistry, Jorge found a job working in a laboratory. He worked under a woman who always challenged him to do his work thoroughly. He remembers her, though, with both fondness and sorrow. Years later, she was kidnapped and murdered along with members of her family because of her political views during the Dirty War, a conflict in the 1970's and 80's between the military dictatorship and guerrilla fighters in which thousands of Argentineans disappeared.

Initially unhappy with his father's decision to make him work, Jorge recalls later in his life that work was a valuable formative experience for him that taught him responsibility, realism, and how the world operated. He learned that a person's self worth often comes from their work, which led him to become committed later in life to promote a just culture of work rather than simply encouraging charity or entitlement. He believes that people need meaningful work in order to thrive. During his boyhood through his priestly ministry, he experienced the gulf in Argentina between the poor and the well off, which left the poor having few opportunities for gainful employment.

At the age of twenty-one, Jorge became dangerously ill. He was diagnosed with severe pneumonia and cysts. Part of his upper right lung was removed, and each day Jorge endured the pain and discomfort of saline fluid pumped through his chest to clear his system. Jorge remembers that the only person that was able to comfort him during this time was a religious sister who had catechized him from childhood, Sister Dolores. She exposed him to the true meaning of suffering with this simple statement: "You are imitating Christ." This stuck with him, and his sufferings during that time served as a crucible for his character, teaching him how to distinguish what is important in life from what is not. He was being prepared for what God was calling him to do in life, his vocation.

Made in the USA
Lexington, KY
28 July 2016